Unbinding

Unbinding

THE GRACE BEYOND SELF

Kathleen Dowling Singh

WISDOM PUBLICATIONS
199 Elm Street
Somerville, MA 02144 USA
wisdompubs.org

Jan Richardson's lines of poetry are freely offered by her from *Circle of Grace*. She maintains a website at janrichardson.com.
Ok-Koo Kang Grosjean's poetry is from *A Hummingbird's Dance*, published by Parallax Press.

Library of Congress Cataloging-in-Publication Data
Names: Singh, Kathleen Dowling, author.
Title: Unbinding: the grace beyond self / Kathleen Dowling Singh.
Description: Somerville, MA: Wisdom Publications, 2017. |
Identifiers: LCCN 2017003559 (print) | LCCN 2017028526 (ebook) |
    ISBN 9781614294610 (ebook) | ISBN 9781614294450 (pbk.: alk. paper)
Subjects: LCSH: Mysticism. | Spirituality—Buddhism. | Spiritual life—Buddhism.
Classification: LCC BL625 (ebook) | LCC BL625 .S5125 2017 (print) |
    DDC 294.3/444—dc23
LC record available at https://lccn.loc.gov/2017003559

ISBN 978-1-61429-445-0   ebook ISBN 978-1-61429-461-0

21 20 19 18 17   5 4 3 2 1

Cover design by Phil Pascuzzo.
Interior set in Arno Pro 12/17.

Contents

CONTENTS

Part Three: Setting the Stage

Part Four: Fools Rush In

Part Five: Surrender

Foreword

Kathleen Dowling Singh's writing is full of grace.

Not only has she written eloquently on grace in her many books on aging, death, and life, but the very stroke of her pen sets the reader on course to experience it firsthand. Her books come alive from the grace in her, and *Unbinding: The Grace Beyond Self* has the same effect. She knows it as an immediate offering, given to each of us whether we recognize it or not. She does not tell us that grace is something practiced, studied, or bestowed, but rather that it is the essence of life itself. She proclaims that we dwell in the sacred at all times.

Having a comprehensive grasp of the inherent wisdom of many spiritual traditions, Kathleen uses this book to dive into one of the Buddha's central teachings on dependent arising, which meticulously unfolds the mental construction of the sense-of-self. She skillfully uses our natural awareness, the only tool that lies beyond all mental obstruction, to help us see through the imaginary world of self and other. Clear seeing coupled with surrender becomes our way forward. We are guided along the way with many practical exercises that reinforce the points she is making but always and foremost we are encouraged forward through the grace of her voice toward the freedom that is ever present.

In *Unbinding*, we are gently led into a deep inquiry and thorough contemplation of the interconnected conditions on which the self is built. Kathleen makes it clear that the point of this journey is to have our own realized understanding of the experience of self-construction so we can abide within these teachings rather than ponder them from a distance. Her frequent admonition to pause and consider the point at hand helps us ground ourselves in that realized truth.

Let us be clear that deconstructing the sense of being separate from the world is not a frivolous or stress-free undertaking—yet when we dedicate ourselves to this journey there is nothing more fascinating or joyful. For many reasons outlined in this book we may find ourselves reluctant to look at who we are, and most of us need a compelling reason for the inquest. To arouse that motivation, Kathleen steers us through the Buddha's four noble truths, where we are directed to explore and accept radical responsibility for how our self-images create life's conflicts. With each insight and revelation about the nature of self comes a partial or, in some cases a total, unbinding of our confiscated attention that has been held captive by our ignorance and misperceptions. Once freed, awareness spreads out beyond space and time where it cannot be confined by our egoic positions.

With the warmth that Kathleen emanates throughout this work, it is of little wonder that she concludes within the expansive embrace of the Heart Sutra. The Heart Sutra has been behind the scenes of this entire book, the gathering storm of grace that permeates every line. It may be difficult to understand how a wisdom teaching that frames the nothing that everything is could simultaneously radiate as the underpinning of life itself, but such is grace. The author allows this paradox to remain a koan for the reader to ponder: everything is intrinsically empty yet the wind blows and the leaves fall.

Reading this book, I am reminded of a saying in the Gospel of Thomas, where Jesus says, "Those who seek should not stop seeking until they find. When they find, they will be disturbed, and when they are disturbed, thereafter they will marvel and come to rest." *Unbinding* is meant to disturb and unsettle our assumptions, provoke inquiry, and nourish our spirits.

Thereafter, may we all be full of wonder and come to repose.

Rodney Smith
Seattle, Washington

RODNEY SMITH is the author of Lessons from the Dying, *as well as other books, and is the founding teacher of Seattle Insight Meditation Society.*

PART ONE

Wise View

1

Unbinding

UNBINDING IS A BOOK FOR MYSTICS. I am not using the word *mystic* in its usual connotation, with images of celestial visions or walks in haloed glory. I'm using the word here in a specific and practical way. A dictionary definition—precise and lovely—describes a mystic as "a person who seeks by contemplation and self-surrender to obtain unity with or absorption into the...Absolute." We could extend that definition to include a person who seeks, by contemplation and self-surrender, to recognize the Absolute as always and already ever-present, the very ground and essence of our being.

In that sense, every sincere practitioner from every wisdom tradition is a mystic. We all practice contemplation and self-surrender out of a deep, grace-engendered longing for the sacred. My intention here is to speak in broad language to all mystics—crossing traditions with words, insights, teachings I've been blessed to receive from many teachers, and views that are useful for practitioners from any lineage. We all want the freedom of sanity and peace, the undefended inclusiveness of love. We all want refuge in grace.

Steadfast and sincere practitioners from any authentic tradition recognize that we share a commonality of blessings: depth, insight, and mutually known experiential referents. We have all tasted awareness beyond self. We also hold in common ripening qualities of wisdom and compassion, love and peacefulness, as grace fills the spaces previously occupied by shallowness and confusion. I no longer think it matters so much what we label ourselves when we meet together—whether Buddhist, Christian, or Hindu, for example—except in terms of honoring and accrediting the insights we can share from our own paths. Together in grace, it doesn't seem to matter how we got here.

Contemplatives have long recognized that the word *God* connotes so much more than "a superior being." Such a notion diminishes what we point to with the word. God refers to infinite Being. It is called the *dharmakaya* in Buddhism. When we meet together, in person or through a book, I use the word *grace* as an ecumenical word denoting *the sacred*, denoting *Being*, denoting *God*. *Grace* seems to be a word sincere practitioners from all traditions can live with, as it turns all our hearts to the light. We all understand the Great Mystery can only be hinted at. Words only point us toward it.

The word *grace* is used throughout this book to speak of that from which we have never for a moment been separate, except in our confusion. *Grace* points to an inconceivable, pervasive, sacred immensity, containing, in the present, the love of every being who ever lived—the love of Jesus, Buddha, the saints and sages, all our ancestors and every departed loved one as well as the love of all those yet unborn.

Unbinding looks closely, almost under a magnifying glass, at the confusions and obstructions that arise in each of us as we incline toward the sacred—or, we could say, as the sacred inclines us toward it. We will look closely at the causes and conditions that create, to whatever degree, our bewildered unease and hesitation—like a startled fawn—before the always open door into the Absolute, the ground of our being. We'll look at what keeps pulling us back into the tight and binding grip of self-reference in spite of grace's welcome out of it, in spite of our heartfelt longing to respond to the invitation.

Whether we're new to practice or our meditation cushions are already well worn, we've all seen the aphorisms and easy answers that float around, advising us to let go of our anxieties, step free of our masks, walk away from our dramas and our penchant for drama creation. There's a market for bumper-sticker platitudes and the feel-good memes of social media. And yet surely, if we could do any of those things as easily as most of the glib words suggest, we would have done so already.

For a long while on our spiritual journey, we're stuck—like flies on flypaper—in ego. In spite of our growing longing for the sacred as grace arises in us, calling us, we keep ourselves stuck through ignorance. Ignorance is our willingness to ignore, to *not* examine or inquire into what's actually going on, what this egoic sense of self actually is. Ignorance supports the suffering—both great and small—that the separate self-sense experiences. It is suffering's supporting condition, the foundation upon which suffering rests.

Ignorance blocks the wisdom that can free us. I can't let go of my anxieties without seeing the causes that create them. I can't step free of my masks without uncovering the seductive pull to keep them in place. I can't simply cease my drama churning until I have some understanding of the dynamics that compel me over and over to continue to create them.

Seeing—actually looking at what's going on—operates at a focused energetic level, with a laser-like intensity of attention. Clear seeing has far more power than the diffuse "spiritual thoughts" we often allow to remain mere platitude. We tend to treat truths glibly; we treat them

5

as if we already know and fully understand their meaning. In doing so we obstruct their potential to actually impact us. We skip the personal implications of truth. In so doing we deny ourselves the great spiritual opportunity of embodying truth.

How many times have you heard people say things such as "God's will be done" or "Mind creates our reality"? Imagine how different our lives would be if we actually lived the meaning instead of mouthing the words. We would live in an utterly different world, already free of suffering. I think often of the impact on us if we were to take Jesus's words to heart and simply "love one another"—a phrase we think we understand.

Conceptualization is easy. Conceptualization, though, is *not* seeing, and it has no transformative value. Seeing is direct experience, direct realization, and it can radically shift both our experience of being and our view. We unbind from limitation through seeing, through direct realization at the level of our own hearts.

MOST OF US HAVE BEEN BLESSED with insights, no matter how fleeting, into all that lies beyond the trapped attention and subsequently limited world of ego. We've been blessed with a longing, ever growing, for a deeper experience of being. Yet most of us spend many of our waking hours solidifying, without questioning, the very sense of egoic self that keeps us feeling separate from the sacred.

We spend most of our days, even as sincere practitioners, in ignorance of the true nature of things, in ignorance of a radiant and always accessible reality, hidden in plain view and available to us in this and every second. Just pause for a moment, if you like. Quiet. Just recognize ever-present awareness. This pausing to quiet is something we don't ordinarily do.

We spend most of our days ignoring the very ground of our being. We remain unaware of the causes and conditions that give rise to the mistaken belief that we are separate from grace and our consequent self-referential and stressful experience of life. Our experience of existence is most often lived trapped and bound, believing in a limited and mistaken sense of the totality of who we are. Endless energy is spent comparing, judging, strategizing, manipulating, preening, and defending our own ego. It's exhausting and stressful. Ultimately, ego is illusory. It's not the truth of our being. We believe ourselves to be so much less than we are.

Although we have the heartfelt desire to free ourselves from that limited sense of existence, ego remains our default position. It remains our default position until we clearly see the suffering, gross and subtle, so endemic in our small self-referential fixation and grow in our willingness to simply surrender the identification. *Unbinding* offers insight into the ways of liberation from that suffering—practical insight, insight that can be practiced, realized, and embodied. And, as is the practice of mystics, it offers ample opportunity for contemplation and self-surrender.

All reverence and honor is due the contributions of every authentic path leading us back to our own essential nature—our Buddha seed, our divine spark, our communion in unconditioned holiness. Honor and reverence for every tradition's contribution arise naturally in all of us. As our commitment to awakening grows and matures, we resonate with every phrasing of wisdom. For the sincere practitioner, each articulation of the truth, from any lineage, can amplify our understanding of every other articulation of the truth.

Krishnamurti, the great twentieth-century Vedic mystic, counseled us to find truth, not through dogma or creed or ritual, but through the understanding of our own mind—through observation. Christian mystics have long recognized, as thirteenth-century St. Bonaventure phrased it, that "unless we are able to view things in terms of how they originate, how they are to return to their end, and how God shines forth in them, we will not be able to understand."

Buddha offered methods or "skillful means"—practices pointing us toward a clarity through which to view the "origination," "return," and the essential nature St. Bonaventure speaks about.

I remember being a fast and wiry kid, loving track and field events—short dashes, long races, running broad jumps, etc. For the life of me though, I couldn't figure out how to do a standing broad jump. I would stand at the line frozen, completely confused as to how to move what to propel my body forward in a leap. I knew what I wanted, but I didn't know how to do it. This frozen paralysis is how many of us feel, imagining a "line" across which we must leap to live in the grace we long for. So many of us feel we don't know "how" to take refuge in grace, to enter it and live from it.

Buddha's insights offer a "how." And so, while *Unbinding* will incorporate the insights and realizations of many wisdom traditions, it rests in great measure on Buddha's sharing of his realized awareness.

In his thirty-three years of teaching and his eighty-four thousand teachings, Buddha's primary message, repeated over and over, was: "I teach suffering and the end of suffering." Out of deep compassion, he wanted to share his wisdom with all suffering beings. He shared so that we all may understand our situation and awaken into the realization of our true nature.

It makes sense for any of us on a spiritual path, no matter which lineage, to pay close and open attention to the wisdom he offered. Rodney Smith, a deeply respected Buddhist teacher, suggests that when we approach these teachings—any sacred teaching—we want our attentiveness to rise to the elevation of the wisdom. We want to mix our mind with the meaning, to allow the wisdom imparted to become our own wisdom realized.

It makes sense for any of us on a spiritual path, again no matter within which lineage, to investigate how Buddha's insights apply to us personally, to investigate their implications in the living of our lives. Buddha's teachings can help every one of us examine the workings of our own minds. They can help us all surrender our identification with the sense of self these dynamics produce and erase the imaginary barrier seemingly separating us from grace.

The profundity of Buddha's gift lies in the access his teachings give us to insight. Insight into the illusory nature of ego can free trapped attention in a way few other paths teach. His offering is the offering of a path of seeing through illusions.

Buddha offered us a template through which to look. He suggested we look carefully at the causes and conditions that give rise to our pervasive egoic sense of separation. "Causes and conditions" is a phrase often used in Buddhist teachings. It refers to the complex confluences that give rise to appearances and experiences. *Cause* refers to a seed, a potentiality. *Condition* refers to circumstances and influences that allow the seed to germinate and flourish. In our discussion in *Unbinding*, the seed we will be exploring is the seed of the "I"-illusion, a cause arisen from previous habituating conditions. The conditions we'll be exploring are the circumstances that provide the fertile ground for egoic self to appear, for the latency to manifest.

Wise view is the Buddhist term for a focused clarity of mind that inquires into the truth as well as the insights and realizations—the wisdom—that arise from the inquiry.

Without wise view our experience of life is an entangled, bewildering, and stressful confluence of conditions that control our body, speech, and mind. Particularly in his teachings on the four noble truths and his teachings on dependent arising—which we will explore in great detail—the template Buddha offers allows us a view leading from confusion to clarity, from unease to ease, from defendedness to love. It is a view that allows unbinding from all that binds us.

We will look at the processes that give rise to—that literally *create*—the egoic sense of self. By "egoic sense of self," "the separate self-sense," "the 'I'-illusion," I am referring to a foundational default experience of life each of us knows intimately. It's the experience of walking an inner dialogue—an ongoing, self-referential commentary—through the world with a sense that this inner dialogue is "me." It's a sense of self, bound within a body, separate from everything else, isolated and alone. It is the sense of self we believe to be the summation and extent of who we are.

We hold that separate self-sense as the definitive statement of our nature, limiting our experience of being in the process. We will look at the craving for becoming "someone," an endeavor undertaken within ignorance. Our craving for becoming, our compulsion to be "somebody," is like the rush to fill the last empty chair in a game of musical chairs.

We *want* to land in a separate sense of self, an "I"-illusion. In our ignorance, we believe anchoring in an egoic sense of self will keep us safe, will keep us from falling into an imagined abyss, into imagined nothingness. We are like the proverbial horse returning to the burning barn.

The poet T. S. Eliot called us all "the hollow men." We uneasily keep reaching for bromides to push down the gnawing intuition, often arising in the midst of a sleepless night, that we don't have a clue what this life, this world, this inexorable march toward death, is about. There's a vacancy, a hollowness, a foundational and unsettling question mark at the very center of our egoic sense of self. Hidden beneath all the assumptions we cling to, ego registers an unwelcome sense that we don't really have a clue.

Rather than plummeting into that fearful unknowing, we engage in an "identity project" defining who we believe ourselves to be. Unconsciously, we believe this will protect us from a fundamental yet inarticulate and deeply repressed recognition of hollowness, of illusoriness.

Each of us has an identity project operating almost around the clock. We use it to protect, through definition and narrative, the tenuous and uneasy egoic sense of self in which our attention is trapped. Our identity project is noisy—endlessly proclaiming what we want, what we believe, who we think we are.

Truth be told, the call of "I" and "me" and "mine" intrigues and seduces us all in every unmindful moment. We're addicted to the sense of an egoic self. We're addicted to continuing the cycle of ignorance, the cycle of conditioned arisings that produces the egoic sense of "I," as blindly as a mouse in a lab cage will just keep pushing that lever for another crummy little pellet.

Our thirst, that craving for becoming, has us in its grasp. Like a puppet master or a programmer of robots, it conditions and determines our experience, our perceptions, our thoughts and emotions. It conditions our very sense of self, that tightly woven fabrication we attempt to throw over the abyss of Mystery. Scared of chaos, scared of not knowing, we use our identity project to try to weave solid ground, try to stitch a seamless narrative we believe to be "me."

This is what we all do when we cling to the small separate self-sense as the extent and reality of our being. This is what we all do when we are not consciously at home in our essence, our true and unlimited nature. A friend once told me he had built walls around himself, "for protection," as he said. With real tears of despair, he talked of how he felt, how paralyzed and stuck and penned in behind the walls, unable to get out and simply *be*.

We all have a strong tendency to get trapped in the web we've woven. Our attention is ensnared and bound within the craving for an egoic self-sense. Buddha taught what he did so that we might release our attention into vaster, unconditioned being. His intention, as is grace's intention, is that we might become unbound, that we might "alight in unbinding," as he said, assuring us that this was possible for each of us. It is our birthright, our privilege, and our purpose to recognize our true nature as grace.

In simple and contemporary terms we will discuss practices that are accessible and eminently usable in our everyday lives, just as we are living them. Dharma—the truth and the path to the truth—works in our culture with the circumstances of our times and with our newly emergent styles of using the gifts of human capacity. We will come to recognize that Buddha's insight was so piercing that the exact same conditioning dynamics that produce the illusion of "I" he witnessed in his mind still arise in our minds today, almost twenty-six centuries later.

Unbinding will offer views and practices that provide a template for looking at what's going on in these minds of ours and will encourage every opportunity to see. A refrain in Buddhism is, "Recognition is liberation." Seeing is liberation. American mystic Martin Luther King, Jr. echoed John 8:32 when he proclaimed: "The truth shall set you free."

My suggestion is to read the book slowly, contemplatively. Note especially where you resonate. Our hearts resonate with what we already know to be true, what we've already realized. Such resonance validates grace's ever-presence within us as wisdom.

There are many suggestions to pause throughout the book. The pauses allow for structured reflection. I write primarily for readers who have already established or are beginning to establish a committed daily practice. The benefit of the suggested exercises of pausing relies upon a daily practice of enough duration to allow attention to be absorbed in awareness. The suggestions presuppose a practice that has begun to train our minds in the clear seeing such stable absorption allows. They presuppose a growing ability to discern that compassion and loving-kindness lead to greater peace both within and around us; that attachment and aversion lead inevitably to tension and confusion, also both within and around us.

If you do not yet have a daily practice, I invite you to consider establishing one. If we long for awareness beyond "self," a daily meditative practice is essential. We can't think our way to awakening.

We charge our phones each day. It is infinitely more important to "charge" our being, connecting deliberately with ever-present grace and inviting grace to work its way with us. A daily practice works to "free" trapped attention, allowing it to remain in what the Surat Shabd Yoga tradition calls "sweet remembrance" of the sacred. With a daily practice, we offer ourselves a growing familiarity with grace as well as with what ninth-century mystic Teresa of Avila called "the three stages of prayer"—recollection, silence, and union.

We will come to know "the prayer of recollection," a deliberate ingathering of our wandering attention. Here, we begin to reclaim the attention that is so often lost in ignorance and inessentials. We begin to experience grace as a reliable refuge free from suffering. We plant our intention to awaken within it, deepening our capacity to surrender all counter intentions within the wisdom of that refuge. We will come to know "the prayer of quiet," entry into the peaceful absorption of silence, where self-reference remains as only a latent wisp. Cooperating with grace's transformative work upon us, as we invite and allow it, we will come to know "the prayer of union." We begin to rest in our own essential nature. It is not other than grace.

It is helpful to end each meditation session with a physical gesture, imprinting stillness within the body. Touch your heart, do a gesture with your hand—perhaps putting thumb and forefinger together or place your palms together in the gesture of prayer. Do whatever works for you. Once you've established a habit of linking meditative stillness and clarity with a bodily reminder as you arise from your practice, whatever gesture you've chosen can be used throughout the day to evoke stillness and clarity. Such a practice enables even a brief pause of inquiry to be of benefit.

I hope you, the reader, will accept each invitation to pause. I hope you'll pause to inquire and contemplate even when there is no suggestion to do so. I hope you'll follow your own heart's direction to pause, to savor and cultivate that with which you resonate.

It is in the pausing and looking that *Unbinding* can become more than simply informational for you. It can become transformational—deepening realizations and expanding view. And this transformational shift with deepening realization and expanding view allows a more expansive sense of identity and more subtle ways of knowing, facilitating further transformation with deepening realization and expanding view. And so it goes, endlessly into mystery's revelation.

In our ignorance-spawned craving for the cherished "I," the egoic self-sense rushes to fill in all the "gaps" of our constant mental churning. The pauses allow insight into the spaciousness we typically miss when unmindful. The poet Naomi Shihab Nye reminds us that "there is so much we overlook, while the abundance around us continues to shimmer."

When we pause, deliberately and intentionally, we allow wisdom a chance to see. We replace our typical habit of allowing ignorance to simply gloss over the surface, filling in the gaps, and imagining—with a lick and a promise—that it understands what's going on. Every sincere practitioner knows the precious transformational shift that arises when we function with wise view, when we clearly see the truth of a teaching for ourselves, when a realized awareness shared with us becomes our own realized awareness.

THE IDEAS EXPRESSED HERE are not, ultimately, mine. They come from Buddha and the yogis and yoginis who awakened within the sophisticated and skillful practices of the tradition he taught. They come from Jesus and the hundreds of thousands of contemplatives who awakened by loving him and following the simplicity of his suggestion to love one another. The ideas come from Rumi, Hafiz, Rabia and the countless mystic poets of Sufism as well as the long lineage of the nondual sages of India—innumerable heroes and heroines who walked the path before us. The ideas come from grace.

Yet the words are mine. The style too is mine. I often return to an insight multiple times, exploring it from different angles and at different levels of depth. Perhaps that comes from the experience of being a mother and knowing full well that the birth of a new being is only possible after waves of gradually widening openings. Perhaps I'm simply a slow learner. Perhaps both.

I am one of the beneficiaries of all those who pointed us toward the sacred. My words are expressed through the prism of my experience and understanding. Use the words here, as you will, for inspiration. Although they are meant ecumenically, translate, if need be, into words that hold more authentic meaning for you. All the words are simply vehicles used so that grace can work upon us.

My prayer is that my particular sharing of this universal message be of benefit. For each of us, may what needs to be seen be seen, may what needs to be healed be healed, and may what can be surrendered be surrendered.

We ourselves can realize Buddha's realizations through contemplation of them and through the application of their meaning in our own experience. Realization takes courage, honest self-reflection, and the working of grace—as both longing and wisdom—within our precious individual manifestation.

Shining a light is revealing. To the degree that we remain steadfast in our intention, our willingness to look—to shine a light—will reveal our already present essential nature. That revelation, the result of such committed contemplation, will also uncomfortably shatter many of our unexamined beliefs, including the ones we most identify with, the ones we most cling to. The experience can be unsettling, disconcerting, even jarring. Fellow mystic Hermann Hesse said this process of revelation and transformation "tastes of folly and bewilderment, of madness and dream, like the life of all people who no longer want to lie to themselves."

With that potential liberative shattering in mind—the consequence of personally opening to the folly, bewilderment, madness, and dream—let me begin with a gentle introduction, an invitation into wise view.

Let's start with some imagery, an imagistic contemplation, with which I hope you resonate.

2

Eddies in the Stream

A SOLITARY WALK IN THE WOODS can deliver any of us to the hushed, enlivened experience of wonder—bare wonder, free from elaboration. As our feet step atop the thick carpet of sheddings returning to the earth, our face registers warmth when narrow rays of sunlight filter their way down through the million-leaved canopy. Thoughts quiet in the stillness of the woods. Self-reference diminishes in the simplicity of our seclusion. We become more present. Attention increasingly *attends*—to the chatter of a squirrel, the snap of a twig crunched underfoot, the scent of moss and native flowers, the refreshment of the ionized air around a nearby stream.

I have been blessed many times to walk through woods on this beautiful planet of ours. These hours of wonder and gratitude and peace gave rise to a spontaneous meditation, one that led to some understanding. It's one I've contemplated often since, letting the imagery wash over me, time and time again.

Let me share this contemplation.

IMAGINE, IF YOU WILL, a small woodland stream, fresh and freely flowing. The atmosphere around it is moist and clean and aerated.

The stream's waves bubble and crisscross, rising and falling, and the rises and the falls make their lovely babbling sounds. The small stream flows along, past the boulders and exposed roots on its banks, over the rocks and stones on its uneven bed—the deposits of a passing glacier a million years ago.

An uneven rock ledge juts out a bit from the water, just enough to create a little waterfall as the stream drops over it.

As the water rushes over the ledge, some is pushed over to the side in the stream level below. It gives rise to a small eddy in an indentation of the bank. The eddy circles, around and around, remaining fixed in its position. It becomes "backwater," while the water of the rest of the stream flows by.

Inside the circle of the eddy, the circular movement continues its swirl, its rounds—over and over and over. Inside the eddy, momentum concentrates and moves inward to the pattern of circling. Imagine, if you will, that attention turns away from the fresh and freely flowing stream and is drawn into the centripetal force of the circular patterning. The eddy is defined by the circular pattern. Imagine, too, that it identifies inside its circled boundary as *something* and as something *separate from* the freely flowing stream.

We can imagine that, with this identification, the eddy checks its circular motion well and often, monitoring it carefully so as to circle well, to remain in the comfort of the familiar. It compares itself to neighboring eddies, judging and evaluating. It imputes itself as separate, as independent, as needing to be protective of its own circularity. It comes to cherish its swirling—the dynamic that creates its tiny universe. It comes to cherish all the debris caught within the swirls with a sense of personal reference about each of the particles trapped inside its muddied orbit.

Its view becomes myopic. It forgets all about the rounded, ancient mountain down which the stream flows. It forgets the centuries of melting snows and summer rains that create the stream, the mass of tree roots and the rutted animal paths that determine the course of the stream as it flows down the sloped terrain and through the woods. It forgets all about the small ledge of stone that creates the waterfall above it. It forgets all the immeasurable causes and conditions that give rise to its appearance.

Not looking—*ignoring*—the eddy assumes itself according to its ignorance. It ignores that its patterning never for a moment holds the same water. It does not look and it does not see that, in each new moment, new water is recruited, unquestioned, into the familiar circling pattern by virtue of its momentum.

Holding itself as eddy only—as an isolated phenomenon—it remains ignorant of the fact that nothing exists independently of the conditions giving rise to it, that all of life leads to each arising. It loses sight of its inseparability from the fleeting co-arising of stream and squirrel and mountain and cloud and wind and planet and galaxy, a snapshot of a moment in cosmic time.

Unaware, not looking, it ignores its fragile impermanence. A small rabbit, a fox, could cross upstream at any moment, dislodging a waterlogged twig at the crest line of the fall, ever so slightly changing the course of the stream. The eddy would be gone in an instant, leaving no trace in the water, as if it were never there.

Unaware, not looking, the eddy clings to the circled fabrication. It ignores its essential nature, never realizing that its separation from the living water is only imagined. Beyond assumed identities and limitations, everything is already interconnected in all aspects.

IT'S CERTAINLY NOT DIFFICULT to recognize ourselves in this metaphor, to recognize ourselves as eddies in the stream. It's not difficult to recognize two similar cases of mistaken identity.

Just as our own fleeting appearance, an eddy is a temporarily stable pattern of continually changing elements. It sustains itself through constant definition—in the eddy's case through its circularity, in our case through our equally circular inner dialogues. Just as in our own fleeting appearance, the eddy is released from self-limitation as formed pattern when it recognizes it is of the same nature as the stream.

Each of us, like every eddy, is an emergent, fleeting phenomenon arisen from immeasurable causes and conditions within which each phenomenon—including our sense of self—is utterly interdependent and empty of inherent existence from its own side. Most of us don't yet realize, much less thoroughly embody, that truth. Contemplating Buddha's insights offers us a chance to deepen our understanding and experience of our true nature.

Attention trapped in a self-only, form-only paradigm becomes constricted. In that constriction it becomes dense. The density of ten thousand colliding thoughts blocks the revelation of the sacred. This is our uncomfortable, congested, and confusing experience when attention is trapped in and confined to egoic consciousness. Grace, on the other hand, is unconfined and boundless. It does not exclude self and form; it does not hold them as other. It embraces them while allowing the expansion of awareness into limitlessness. It recognizes everything as of the same nature.

The problem with our egoic self-sense is that, believing it to be the final statement of who we are, we cling to it. We fixate on it and perpetuate it, allowing the precious gift of our attention to remain trapped and bound within it. This is not to suggest that "I" don't exist at all.

Clearly I, and all of us, exist but—until awakening—we exist ignorant of our true nature. After releasing our attachment to who we have believed ourselves to be, we still have a grateful, humble, and noble awareness of existing as an individual manifestation of grace. We still brush our teeth and hopefully hold doors open for each other. A sense of our individual manifestation remains necessary not just to survive but to be an offering to others, an agency of kindness and compassion. This is our humanity. The capacity to respect, appreciate, and live our full humanity arises spontaneously when attention is released from confinement within the "I"-illusion.

We are sleepwalking when the attention of awareness is trapped within a "self," a single point of egoic reference. We are lost in a dream. Awareness of existing as an individual manifestation of grace, on the other hand, is an awakened view. Awakening is a growing illumination. Grace increasingly shines in and through us as the fog of who we had believed ourselves to be dissipates, as the congested density thins into clear spaciousness.

Awareness is an endless continuum. It extends from trapped to free, from confusion to clarity, from bound to unbound. Our clinging to an egoic self-sense keeps us in a limited point of reference on that endless continuum.

I think often about the limitations I accept and allow to be placed upon my own experience of being. Years ago my family lived in the Virgin Islands. When I traveled there to visit I knew the clear-watered, frangipani-scented paradise that awaited. I flew from a big city airport, set in a treeless, littered, wasteland of rubble with air that choked your throat. As I sat in the airport waiting for the plane, looking at the city through the windows, I would think about the people who lived and died there—who had never once left its bleakness, who never knew the beauty that lay beyond the crumbling concrete. It seems to me that such are the limitations we live in when all we know of life is the egoic self.

We misunderstand who we are. As we free our fixated self-reference, as we unbind ourselves from ignorance, ego's functional capacities remain, but attention is liberated into a far greater continuum of being—our essential nature.

AS WE EXPLORE some of Buddha's teachings in *Unbinding*, we will recognize that he shared them so that we ourselves might *unbind*. By "unbind," I mean free our attention from the typically unconscious dynamics that ensnare it in ignorance—particularly in the identification with an egoic sense of self. Unbinding refers to the liberation of trapped attention, releasing it into awareness, into grace.

Exploring these teachings, we can come to clearly see the interplay of dynamic, mutually patterning causes and conditions that give rise, in each moment, to each of our individual and separate self-senses. We'll look at how endless possibility converges in a single apparent actuality. Buddha's insights outline the dynamics, the pattern-making, of the sense of "I" we cling to.

We'll look at the liberating power of wisdom. It sees through the fabrications and the rippling reactivity produced by these dynamics. Seeing, clear seeing, allows unbinding. We need to see just enough to know that we ourselves create our existential unease in a blind acceptance of habit.

My grandmother lived with us as I was growing up. Every time a boy came to pick me up for a date, my grandmother would take one look at him, roll her eyes, and in a rather loud whisper announce, "That one knows more than his prayers." Seeing clearly all the ways we each have allowed "more than our prayers" to hijack this precious human life, we shift into greater freedom.

Seeing clearly breaks the spell of ignorance. It breaks down the walls of our self-referential paradigm. As it does, grace and our attention rush together in mutual embrace—merging in interpenetration and recognized unity. Catholic mystic Thomas Keating has observed, "The contemplative life, already present within us through the Divine Indwelling, waits for our consent." Our exploration—deep, honest, personal exploration—of the factors functioning in our own minds allows us to see through their conditioning force in such a way that our attention is finally "unbound" enough to give that consent.

This book won't be particularly helpful to anyone if we limit our understanding to the merely conceptual. It does not benefit us particularly, as sincere practitioners, as mystics, to engage in hoarding more theories or complex conceptualizations. We don't need to pack more into the backpacks we lug around on our spiritual journey, hoping that someday we will have gathered "enough." The only "enough" that needs to be said is the "Enough!" to suffering and limitation and confusion.

The benefit of sharing all these teachings arises for us *practically*—in practice, with engagement. We need to pause and explore, inquire into and see, the cyclic and patterned arising of conditions in our own minds and the byproduct of egoic self they give rise to. It is through such contemplation and consequent self-surrender that we come to recognize the impossibility of ever for a moment being separate from grace.

To that end we'll begin by exploring some of the many ways in which we defend who we think we are. This defensive stance remains in many of us sincere practitioners, even though we've been fairly warned that our sense of being—now bound in self-reference—will be transformed in the process of awakening. We'll peel away some of the layers of defendedness and ignorance to expose the naked tension in which our imagined self lives. Through exploration and contemplation, we will get a sense of the pervasive unease of ego and the lack of a single reliable, unchanging refuge in the self's world.

As we get a clearer view of the tension inherent when attention is trapped in ego, our commitment to the constant defense of our imagined boundaries diminishes. We reevaluate our priorities, our direction, and our longings. Hopefully together we will each experience even a slight shift in our defendedness. Such a shift can begin to transform our intention from one of self-protectiveness to one of self-surrender.

We can find liberation beyond only form and beyond only self when we work with wisdom, when we allow grace's wisdom to work upon us. We will look at and work with *wise view*, with *clear seeing*. Clear seeing breaks the spell of ignorance. We'll look at the ease that clear seeing brings. It enhances our capacity for and our willingness to surrender. It leads, eventually, to *joy* in surrender. And finally, we'll look at where surrender lands us—the magnificent life of a conscious manifestation of the sacred.

Using Buddha's teachings, as well as the hints and guidance of the saints and sages of our rich, many-faceted wisdom heritage, we can engage practical and skillful means to become "stream enterers," to allow the eddies we've imagined ourselves to be to merge into the divine flow.

3

A Liberating View

ANY ONE OF US who has been called by grace to awaken recognizes that there is much beyond only self, much beyond a world of only form. Grace's clarion call spoke our name. We heard it and responded. Even so, even as sincere practitioners, in our moment-by-moment experience, there's the all-too-frequent obstruction of the "self" we still believe to be the extent and reality of our being. The obstruction of the separate self-sense pops up often—and often endures without our notice, without our mindful attention—like a giant cardboard cutout of "me" that blocks the view of anything beyond it.

Hopefully each of us has had at least one long, deep, and honest reflection, recognizing how lost we feel in this sense of separation, how alienated and tense, how lonely and discouraged. We wander so far from grace.

We may have wondered how we lost touch with such vast aspects of our own being—the sacred aspect, the interconnected aspects, the true aspects, the open and undefended aspects. In moments of clarity, we're stunned to see how bound we've been in smallness, how distant from authentic dignity and how distant from peace.

Grace arises in us as love, compassion, and all the other noble qualities of our awakened humanity. When it arises as wisdom, we recognize how persistently stuck we are in identifying with only an eddy in the stream. When we have not yet fully cultivated and embodied the glimpses we've had of realized awareness, we assent to this limitation. As we come to see more clearly, we may shake our head at the perversity that keeps us going back behind the very wall obstructing our recognition of grace.

It might be helpful to pause for a short while here to examine your experience of being in this very moment. Take a deep breath, relax your shoulders, and just pause. Check in. Explore. Poke around.

Is there any sense of feeling separate or tense? Check if your experience of being feels bound or contracted. Is there a density to it or a clarity? Does it feel congested or spacious, light?

Inquire, with focus and sincerity, what is calling you to awaken. We can ask ourselves: what is the nature of my longing? We each have had glimpses and tastes of grace, of the sacred. Without judgment, simply note the thoughts and the powerful habituated patterns that function as obstructions to the experience of grace. We each have many of them. Take the time to note some. When we do notice an obstructing belief, it's helpful to inquire into our motivation for believing it.

Spend some time recognizing that the awareness inquiring is *beyond* the obstruction. And rest in that mind of open inquiry for a while. Simply rest in it.

Something beyond the bound, contracted state asks the question. Something beyond the ignorance that keeps us bound in ego observes what the asking reveals. That "something beyond" is wisdom, the clarity in which the question is asked, the clarity that realizes what is revealed. Wisdom is an aspect of grace and one of the always-open doors to it.

Rest in grace for a few moments. You will note that it has no tension. It is always content. Rest in that ease and contentment for a few minutes more, enjoying its respite.

You may find, as you end your pause, a tendency to collapse the ease and spaciousness of the pausing—a tendency to return, even if only slightly, to contraction and the tight grip of egoic self. Note the tendency if it arises. This will allow you to become increasingly mindful of the operation of the tendency. To the degree you're able, surrender the urge to follow the tug back into such a limited and mistaken sense of who you are. We can grow in our capacity to joyfully offer up the urge in the name of awakening. Offering up the urge in the name of awakening is the essence of surrender.

A SIGNIFICANT INVESTIGATION, one well worth undertaking with commitment, is inquiry into exactly what it is that keeps us returning to such a contracted identity. What causes us, heirs to grace—itself a boundless stream of frequencies—to keep turning the dial back to the single, fixed point of "me"? What keeps pulling attention back into ego?

Perhaps it hasn't fully dawned on us that the commitment to awaken is a total one. Perhaps part of us still holds the thought that our ego can make it through the spiritual journey intact, unharmed, and hopefully more "comfortable." Perhaps part of us still holds who we believe ourselves to be as an unquestionable truth, such an obvious "given" that inquiring into that most basic of assumptions would be pointless. I can see in myself how, because self-reference is so ubiquitous—shading everything—I can become blind to the obscuring shadow it casts. This blindness, often willful, is the very definition of ignorance.

Awakening requires that we see through the limiting and distorting—ultimately illusory—sense of self to which we so cling and which we so cherish. The cost of our essential nature is the surrender of the inessential egoic self. In Viktor Frankl's words: "What is to become light must endure burning."

We may have had deep and prolonged experience in the presence of the sacred, merged within the force of that love, the awe of such radiance and majesty. Have we deeply and thoroughly recognized that there is no "I" present in those moments? Have we fully taken in the implications of that recognition?

We may have realized the shocking absence of the self with which we typically identify when we've gone to look for it with steadied and intended mind. The realization of that shocking absence of what we thought was there can blow apart all previous notions, spinning us out of ego's gravitational pull and into unboundedness, into free fall. Upon arising from that realization, have we seen what it is that pulls us back into the orbit of self-reference?

Are we mindful of the compulsion to grab onto an identity, a separate sense of self, to break the fall—as if that identity, that separate sense of self, had a solidity that could break? Do we even notice the movement out of clarity into a confused fog? Do we notice the profound collapse in our being from vastness to a tiny point of tension—far too small and cramped to contain life? These are beneficial discernments.

A friend once described his experience of moving from still and utter lucidity to what could be called "the burden of self." He said he rose from sleep one morning, clear and silent. Standing there by the side of the bed, he said he felt the sharp bombardment of remembrance of the day's plans. He felt the onslaught of emotional reactions to the schedule of the day and the decades-old narratives that shaped his emotional reactions. He said he felt the weight as he, with such rapidity, reassumed the noisy burden of ego.

As practitioners do we note the burdensome weight we consent to carry when attention moves from awareness beyond self back to self-reference? When we do become aware of the congested heaviness—especially when it's juxtaposed with the utter lightness of being beyond self—we can begin to acknowledge the subtle suffering that permeates every moment of self-reference.

It is by unmindfully assenting to an "I"-illusion that we return to the closed paradigm of self, trading the stream for the eddy. It is most often a slippery, thoughtless slide back in. We need to understand the dynamics that got us lost and continue to get us lost in an imagined sense of separate self.

The "I"-illusion arises inevitably as an automatic, predictable byproduct of an unexamined, habituated interplay of conditions. It arises from the humming, buzzing conditions of life-in-form that create the separate sense of self as an overtone, a harmonic.

We can think of an intensive care unit in a hospital with all of its machinery for life support. Together, the devices can help uphold the *appearance* of life. But if taken too far into pointless medical heroics, such a situation can mercilessly mimic a life, perpetuating something that would not exist without the machinations. The egoic sense of self exists much like this—as an illusion of an existing life.

The egoic self arises from a confluence of conditions as much as a mirage arises from a confluence of conditions of heat and light rays and eyes and brain. The egoic sense of self—experienced as "me," experienced as real—is, upon close examination, as insubstantial and illusory as the mirage.

"Self," a fabrication as we shall see, only lives tentatively and, so, needs constant confirmation and affirmation. The thought "I" constantly reasserts itself. And we, in ignorance, subscribe to it over and over again. It's like those unwanted emails that just keep coming unless we deliberately go through the procedure to unsubscribe. We keep resubscribing to the "I"-illusion, ignoring the underlying processes that keep churning the illusion into becoming.

We won't be free within any tradition until we see this clearly and until we acknowledge the suffering of our entrapment in the unexamined dynamics of our thoughts and reactivities. Exploring the interplay of the conditions that gives rise to our familiar sense of self offers a liberating view.

Within a closed system of exclusive identification with the conditions of life-in-form, the egoic self-sense along with suffering arises— snared within its confines. It's like being trapped inside a washing machine on the "normal" cycle, battered again and again in the rotation. We try to ignore or to anesthetize ourselves to the uncomfortable reality of the situation. I'm reminded of an observation I heard years ago from the Chilean mystic Oscar Ichazo, who said that most of humanity is so anesthetized we actually believe ourselves to be happy.

Much of what we often term *happiness* in Buddhist view is actually just "changing suffering." Think of standing for a few hours in a long line, for example, and the relief we feel in finally sitting. Think of then sitting for a few long hours wishing to find relief in standing and getting a chance to stretch our legs. Think of how good the air conditioning feels when we enter a restaurant after walking through a steamy parking lot to get there. Or how good going outside again feels momentarily after we've shivered in the restaurant's cold. All of this is "changing suffering"—not genuine happiness at all.

Because the only mind we can liberate is our own mind, ours is the mind we explore. We can ask ourselves what is my own resistance to paying attention, to simply being present and seeing? What's going on beneath the surface of my assumptions? Where am I afraid to look? What am I afraid to find? What do I not wish—or do not feel ready or willing—to acknowledge? What suffering do I simply *tolerate*?

Pause now, if you wish, and examine what arises in your own mind with those questions.

THE DYNAMICS THAT PRODUCE THE EGO are held together by ignorance and habit. To ignorance, the paradigm of ego and its world is a closed system. Without wisdom, there's no exit from that world of stress and defendedness and confusion, no exit through the boundaries ignorance has posited. Attention is bound within its confines.

Self and the conditions giving rise to it recoil from the boundaries they create. The thought of stepping beyond these boundaries threatens the system. Even contemplating "beyond the boundaries" risks destabilization of "self" and the conditions creating the egoic sense—as we may have already witnessed and experienced in our own spiritual practice.

Where self recoils, grace assures. It offers peace; it offers fearlessness. Grace works upon and within us as wisdom, as awareness unencumbered by self-reference. It can open the old, tight paradigm, expanding attention's borders by orders of magnitude through the embracing and liberating force of love. Grace can burn through those fabricated boundaries with clear-seeing wisdom.

We won't be free without wisdom. We won't experience freedom or sanity or our own ripening goodness until we see through—by grace and by intention, by contemplation and self-surrender—the patterned dynamics of the "I" creation. Our attention will remain as trapped as the eddy within its circular pattern.

Pause again for a moment, if you will. Recollect the tensions and confusions that have plagued your peace of mind lately. Recall them. Recall the feelings in your body, the emotions that accompanied them. Recognize the difference between the physical/emotional tension and peaceful sanity, the difference between the unease of self-reference and the ease of self-forgetfulness. This recognition is meaningful. The recognition is discerning wisdom.

Rest for a moment in the clarity, however great or small, that dawns with that recognition. Just stay for a minute and rest in the recognition of the difference between unease and ease, contraction and limitless-ness. Rest in discernment. Discerning wisdom is peaceful sanity.

Unlike the view from egoic self—which is to say, from ignorance—discerning wisdom is undistorted; it is a deep knowing. Every time such a realization arises from clear seeing, we want to hold it as inde-scribably precious. We want to tend it like the last glowing ember on a planet where fire has, but for this ember, become extinct. It is a blessing.

4

The View from Wisdom

WISDOM RECOGNIZES THE SUFFERING that arises when we're trapped in the small eddy of self, trapped in a world of only self and only form, imagining ourselves separate from our own vastness and beauty. Wisdom, the nature of grace—from which we are always and already inseparable—sees what's so.

The simple practice of pausing for the purpose of seeing what actually is true in each moment works to retrain our minds. Practiced often throughout the day, it can reverse our habitual tendency to *not* look closely, to be willing to ignore. It can retrain our habitual tendency to turn away, even if we do look, from what we see and the implications of what we see.

Pausing allows us to become aware of the gaps in our narrative. These gaps are frightening to the egoic self-sense. They reveal a seeming abyss of mystery, the abyss over which we attempt to throw that woven fabrication—"me." Our inner dialogue attempts to fill those gaps, creating a sense of continuity that is our primary locus of self-reference. Ego is a fabrication, an illusion. We can unbind from it.

For those intent on awakening, the gaps revealed in pausing are oases of truth and sanity, tastes of our essential nature. Annie Dillard, the nature poet and mystic, noted: "The gaps are the thing. The gaps are the spirit's . . . home, the altitudes and latitudes so dazzlingly spare and clean that the spirit can discover itself like a once-blind man unbound."

Ignorance is wont to skate quickly over the gaps. Ignoring the gaps allows ignorance to continually acquiesce to the assumption of self. The "I"-illusion is ignorance with a nametag. It only arises in the absence of mindful attention, in the absence of wisdom and clarity.

Pausing and looking allow wisdom. Ignorance and wisdom do not coexist. In wisdom, the "I"-illusion ceases to convince. The wisdom that arises when we pause to see can give us brief refuge from the storm.

To the degree that—from ignorance—we misconstrue reality, reality will compensate. Reality always compensates, sooner or later, as our cherished illusions inevitably bump into the truth. In Buddhism reality's compensation for our obliviousness to it is called *dukkha*, often translated as "suffering." Dukkha is the storm from which we seek refuge.

The word *dukkha* certainly encompasses the intense aspects of suffering we know in a human life—death, loss, grief, disease, disfigurement, war, violence, and hate. Dukkha, though, also includes all of the dissatisfaction, unease, tension, stress, and struggle that color our lives, even lives marked by health and stability and privilege. Dukkha is the malaise we experience as our ignorance grates against the truth. It is uncomfortable to constantly go against what's so. It's a losing battle.

Dukkha is not an external condition. It is not a punishment. It is the subjective experience of a separate self-sense living at a far remove from reality. The suffering we experience when trapped in exclusive self-reference is the consequence of a mistaken sense of identity and the desires of that identity. These desires are strong enough to cause stress and unease—to upset our egoic selves—but they have no power to control what's real and what's true, either in this moment or around the next bend in the road.

I will use the word *suffering* here in *Unbinding*. Please, when it is used, remember the wider range of association and connotation, the wider range of human experience, in the word *dukkha*. *Suffering*, here, will refer to the continuum of turmoil—from the screams of any profound anguish to the sigh of the slightest uneasy egoic contraction.

THE VIEW FROM WISDOM holds the realized awareness of the four noble truths and Buddha's teachings on dependent arising.* These teachings offer us insights. Exploring and contemplating them leads to our own recognition of how bound and limited we are when we identify as an eddy in the stream. It is of immeasurable benefit to make these realized understandings our own understandings. We come to realize that our attention is subject to the conditions that give rise to the "I"-illusion. And attention is subject to the uneasy consequences of those conditions for as long as we allow the unexamined identification to continue.

The four noble truths were the teachings Buddha first taught. They are the cornerstone of the authentic path he shared. They offer the view from wisdom.

---

*These teachings were expounded by Buddha as *pratītyasamutpāda*. *Pratītyā* means "because of" or "dependent upon." *Samutpāda* means "arising" or "origination." Consequently, in English, the teachings go by various names. Among them are dependent co-origination and dependent co-arising. I've chosen the simplest form: dependent arising.

Buddha's teachings can be beneficially mined for decades, and hundreds of thousands of practitioners have done just that. The teachings are vast, complex, and subtle. Buddha, while warning us against the ego's desire to quickly feel that it has understood the teachings, said that without contemplating and penetrating these truths we will not find liberation from suffering.

We may not have Buddha's level of insight, or perhaps not even the nuanced level of insight of the legions of monastics studying and practicing and contemplating for decades. Buddha warned of the "dust in our eyes." This is the "dust" of worldly concerns. It can cloud the view of householders such as ourselves—earnest practitioners who are also engaged in the world. Staying mindful of Buddha's warning, though, we can remove the clouds of dust with diligence, with sincerity and conscientiousness and noble intention. We can balance that dusty deficit with the benefit of having, as householders, a rich field of relationships, demands, and pace in which to practice.

With diligence even a rudimentary understanding of the teachings of the noble truths and dependent arising—internalized and applied—can bring much benefit in our release from the tight grip of self. The teachings offer a transformative view. Even in their simplest form, they provide a template through which to mindfully observe the dynamics that give rise to suffering. We just need to see enough to break the spell.

In Buddha's teachings on the four noble truths, the reality of our situation can be presented in stark simplicity. We only need to see the four truths for ourselves. We only need to make them our own realized understanding. In Buddha's insight into dependent arising, there are twelve mutually conditioning conditions to which he suggested we pay attention. To see and know any one of them can lead to the cessation of the cycle's continued churning of all twelve. We can make these complex teachings simple. What's *not* simple is all that it takes to get us to want to see—to pause and to actually look.

The insights that Buddha presented were not offered as theory or as a set of beliefs to adopt. They were offered as a truth for each of us to experience, a welcome to come and see for ourselves. It only takes seeing. We only need to fully see the arising of self to enter the stream of Being.

The possibility for each of us to benefit from these teachings, intended for anyone from any tradition, is widened when we allow the insights to steep within us. We can hold them as hints and inspiration, as points of exploration, as view-shifters and paradigm-expanders. We want to extrapolate their meaning and apply our understanding in the lives we are living. Paradoxically, we need to make the teachings very personal so that we can unbind ourselves from taking everything personally, as is the "I"-illusion's habit.

And so, with diligence, sincerity, conscientiousness, and noble intention may we attain the realizations of Buddha's teachings, as he hoped we would in the teaching of them.

IN VERY SIMPLE FORM, the four noble truths that Buddha invited us to see for ourselves are these:

1. The first noble truth is the truth of suffering. Suffering, gross and subtle, exists. It is the very texture of our unexamined, unfree experience of existence, of life identified only with form and an egoic sense of self. The experience is of almost continuous unease, limitation, fear, distress, and a sense of separation and alienation.

2. The second noble truth is the truth of the origin of suffering. It can be seen, if we are willing to look, that suffering arises from causes that are dynamic and patterned and hidden beneath a fog of ignorance. We can trace the origin of suffering to the dependently arising conditions that churn out a grasping, seemingly separate sense of self.

3. The third noble truth is the truth of the cessation of suffering. The cessation of suffering, this dissatisfying and unfree experience of existence, is possible for each and every one of us. It is our birthright, our precious gift, and our life's most meaningful task.

4. The fourth noble truth is the truth of the path. There are skillful practices in every authentically transformative tradition that create the conditions for the cessation of suffering.

PART TWO

The Conditions of Self

5

The Tight and Binding
Grip of Self

AS OUR WILLINGNESS TO LOOK and to be with what is—as it is—grows, what is revealed is suffering. We come to see the basic insecurity of the human experience.

The deep, unmediated, nonconceptual realization of the first noble truth—the truth of suffering—demands our experiential honesty. Contemplation is a necessity, a foundation for the realization. Our own thorough realization of the first noble truth touches us, sobers us, and opens our hearts. Our understanding, our experience, our sense of identity, and our priorities can be transformed within the heart's still and clear seeing.

Let's examine together our most habitual experience of being—the truth of suffering.

Our egoic sense of self binds us tightly—perhaps more tightly than we usually recognize. As we explore and contemplate Buddha's teachings, we can come to see the conditions that give rise to this sense of self. The egoic self-sense is an ever-present harmonic of the mutual interplay of these conditions, a seed always ready to ripen in their field.

We come to recognize that these conditions, when unexamined, function to maintain the illusion of that separate self-sense. Their ongoing dynamic keeps churning out a trapped and bound experience of existence. When operating behind the veil of ignorance, these mutu-ally conditioning dynamics build momentum and a crisscrossing ener-getic web. Our unmindful experience of who we think we are—the egoic sense of self—is birthed and sustained in their interplay. Our attention is caught in their web. The ongoing dynamics keep atten-tion increasingly bound as surely as a spider wraps a web-captured fly.

It will be immeasurably helpful for us to recognize this, to *see* it, to *know* it to be so for ourselves. Until we have a clear sense of the tight and binding grip of self, we have little to no intention to free our attention from it.

LET'S EXPLORE the first noble truth—the truth of the pervasive unease of the "I"-illusion, that bound and fixated referent. We want to bring the truth of suffering into close focus, allowing no fogginess or distortion where ignorance might work its way.

For such clear seeing, we need a concentrated mind capable of intent and stable inquiry. Such a concentrated mind is silent—still and unmoving, devoid of self-referential chatter. The Catholic mystic Thomas Merton recognized in his own practice that, "In silence we face and admit the gap between the depths of our being, which we consistently ignore, and the surface which is untrue to our own reality."

A steadfast practice—our cooperation with grace—cultivates the capacity to remain in silence in formal meditation and deepens our capacity to ingather our attention throughout the day. It is that capac-ity to quickly return to silenced concentration that we are employing in our frequent pauses as we engage in inquiry here together.

Even short bursts of focused inquiry benefit. They poke holes in the veil of ignorance and effect a transformative shift, no matter how slight, at the energetic level. As grace starts to make its presence known more insistently, intention and the stability of freed attention become our gifts of spirit. They lead to subsequent insights and ever more profound and thorough realizations. We can begin to experience an endless awakening. In our own being, we come to know deep transformative shifts of both direction and view as well as an increasing sense of sanity, spaciousness, and subtlety.

Except in our greatest moments *in extremis,* most of us typically don't acknowledge the truth of suffering. Even students of Buddhist teachings who could repeat the four noble truths in their sleep often don't acknowledge the truth of suffering at a level of sustained, focused, and embodied depth.

We can voice our objections to "the truth" of suffering. Admittedly, it sounds depressing. It can sound a bit out of balance as a general statement about our lives. We can claim, and rightly so, that we've experienced much happiness. We can cite moments of merging in love, of at-one-ment with nature, the joy of movement and developed skill, the simple contentment of kindness and human connection. What we fail to note in our insistence that "life isn't *all* suffering" is that in none of the examples of happiness is there any sense of "I." No "I" to be found when we merge in love, when we feel at one with nature, when we experience grateful fulfillment. No "I" to be found at all.

Suffering arises with the "self" we believe we are. The quotidian experience of being stuck in an egoic sense of self that takes everything personally, that reacts to everything personally, that blames and grabs and never relaxes is one that we ignore. Stressed contraction is endemic in the human condition when our daily life, with its several million thoughts, endless mood changes, and almost constant bodily tension, operates under and in adherence to the sway of ignorance.

43

We don't acknowledge the unease of "self" consistently, completely, and categorically.

The reality that we live almost continuously in a state of stressed contraction is something that most of us simply don't pay attention to. Accepting stressed contraction without question or investigation, we keep it subliminal. We assent to basic unease in a way. We acquiesce to it and allow it mindlessly. Most of us don't give a second thought to it, accepting it—without radically close examination—as natural and inevitable, as a "given."

We don't attend to that white-noise backdrop of tension in our life, just as the smog in Los Angeles or the poisons in our food or the consequences of systemic racism were not attended to for decades. We simply accepted these conditions until we woke up to the truth of the situation. May we all quickly wake up to the truth of the situation of living within a sense of self ignorant of its true nature. Life is short. Our breaths are numbered.

Even as meditators or contemplatives our attention most often skirts on the very surface of appearances, oblivious to the basic insecurity of the human experience when lived without mindful attention. Without mindful attention, we exist in the mind's imagination, far from reality. Unmindfully, we "live" in whatever story we've been telling ourselves in the day's or hour's current chapter.

We don't look deeply enough or long enough to see the tension, the unease, underlying our every moment within the burden of self. We resist touching that truth. The very resistance is a form of suffering.

BUDDHA POINTED OUT that we have four "perversions of view," four basic misconceptions about the reality of our human situation. We think of the self as constant, we think of it as pleasant. We have an unquestioned conviction in its reality and we allow it to attract our attention.

The first of these "perversions of view" is constancy. Ordinarily, we tend to hold "I" and "me" as constant. We simply assume that each time the self we believe ourselves to be is referenced it's the same self. Without analysis we assent to the illusion of constancy. Have we ever really deeply examined that assumption?

This mistaken belief in the constancy of "I" and "me" is an obstruction, blocking clear seeing. The "I"-illusion is always newly fabricated, newly conditioned, newly churned into being by ever-changing arisings and circumstances, as we will explore. The sense of "being a self" remains the same—"I'm me"—but we place it, like a reused Post-it, on a continuum of constantly morphing phenomena.

I, the meditator, used to rise from meditation and quickly flash into I, the angry mother, yelling at my kids for making noise or messing up the house while I, the meditator, was meditating. I still flash back and forth in various self-identifications without ever noticing the inconstancy.

We can all think of our own examples: victim, savior, avenger, seducer, betrayer, winner, loser, etc. We've all played many of these often contradictory roles. Ask yourself, what roles have I played? Which one is "me"? Do I describe myself as a constant entity? Is that how I think of my "self"? What are the unique words I use in my personal assent to the constancy of "me"? It is helpful to look.

The second perversion of view, basic misapprehension about the nature of our egoic self, is this: We respond to the experience of self as pleasant. We do this even when the thoughts about self might not be pleasant. In other words, even judging or berating ourselves, we tend to find pleasant comfort in the illusion of having any kind of self-sense at all. Curiously, although the *content* of "I" is as varied as there are beings, the *sense* of "I" is the same in each of us. It pleases us to have one.

Each of us knows that self-sense as our default position. Our imagined boundaries seem to hold promise of consistency and safety in a world of so much "other." They seem to offer a defense, a fortress protecting us from chaos. Without mindful attention, we like to imagine ourselves as comfortable and secure, snuggled up inside the fortress walls.

The "I"-thought is our most frequent and pervasive thought. Our separate self-sense is familiar. We tend to hold it as our comfort zone. That comfort zone, no matter how limiting or deadening, is one we're afraid to step beyond. We're often fearful of transition, of risk, and redefinition. We don't "do" change easily; it brings us to the edge of our conceptually known world.

Egoic self views the experience of not-knowing as unpleasant or threatening and backs away. Having recoiled from investigation and inquiry, attention too often simply returns to the illusion with which it's so well acquainted. Perhaps we can notice that in our own minds as we approach views that may be unsettling or new to us in our discussion here. It's helpful to notice our resistances.

Even after we have begun to respond to grace's call to expand beyond only self, we often tumble back and cling to the familiarity we unconsciously deem pleasant. One of the most powerful definitions of sin I've ever heard—free of guilt and shame and self-recrimination—is from the Russian mystic G. I. Gurdjieff. He described sin as that which we do to stay asleep after we've already chosen to follow our longing for awakening. This attribution of "pleasant" to the egoic sense of self has an opiate quality, keeping us in befogged confusion. It is a deeply rutted, known and familiar, mental habit.

Can you touch the very personal way in which you hold your sense of self as basically a pleasant phenomenon, a seemingly comfortable terra firma for all experience? Can you recognize it as your default position? No matter how much kindness or humility or compassion or generosity we have cultivated, this default still holds—and always will hold—"me" as the most cherished center of the universe.

It would be helpful to take a little time to look into and recognize this in your own mind. Just pause for a moment to notice the familiarity of the thought: "me." Note what feeling tones of "pleasant" might arise for you within the thought. Is there a sense of safety in that known world? Spend some time noting. Notice what you might not yet be willing or able to surrender of that comfort. Just note the resistance and the experience of resisting.

Then note the awareness in which the noting is occurring. Step back into that awareness and simply rest in it for a few minutes.

The third perversion of view is about the nature of the self, the habit of unexamined conviction. We believe that our self exists exactly as we conceive of it and perceive it. We believe it to be real. We believe it to be a true and definitive statement of who we are. Rarely, outside of formal practice, do we intentionally question those conceptions and perceptions. Rising from meditation, we often simply return to default—to recycled thoughts and habituated reactivity. The notion that it might be fruitful or revelatory to question our most fundamental assumption is an insight outside of self's repertoire, outside of self's field of vision.

What are your particular assumptions about the nature of the self you believe yourself to be? How unsettling is the notion it might be illusory? How unsettling is the notion it might be mistaken, a limiting distortion?

Let yourself be unsettled, if that's what arises. The stance of inquiry is wisdom. Its nature is clarity—like the sky. Buddhist teacher Pema Chödrön reminds us that a feeling like "unsettled" is like weather passing through the sky. Open to "unsettled," resting in the sky-like nature of wisdom. "Unsettled" can't hurt us. It's likely that it indicates something we might learn or something that needs our tender compassion.

Finally, the fourth perversion of view, the last fundamental misconception about our human situation, has to do with finding the arising of the egoic self—the "I"-illusion—energetically *attractive*. Our thoughts and tendencies are conditioned to relate to it as a compelling and addictive attractor. Without mindfulness or diligence, we allow our "I"-illusion to function like a powerful magnet. In a heartbeat, as we've witnessed many times in both formal and informal practice, it can pull attention away from boundaryless awareness and back into bounded limitation. It calls to us, and unexamined, habituated attention follows its lead, like a hopeful puppy looking for a treat. It has a powerful gravitational force, drawing us into a tiny, eddied orbit. It's seductive.

Without analysis, we cling to our false belief in the separate self-sense as refuge. Without analysis, we assent to the illusion that who we believe ourselves to be has a reality, that it knows what it's doing, and that somehow it will finally manage to choreograph the permanent pleasure we seek.

I can see in myself how the "I"-thought arises so unmindfully, so robotically. Watch in your own mind. No judging—just seeing, just noting. There is such a strong pull to return to self-reference, to the mistaken belief that this is real, this is "me." Our attention has been caught in it for so long it feels like home.

Ordinary mind has a tendency to believe the oft-repeated lie. It's important to understand the dynamics that create—and sustain—the illusion of "self" and the suffering that ensues.

EACH OF THE FOUR perversions arises from ignorance, from not attending to what is actually so. A great percentage of our experience is one of believing the sense of self to be constant, pleasant, real, and attractive. These unexamined beliefs have heft—they have weight and power. And thus, questioning our underlying misconceptions meets with a strongly habituated unconscious resistance.

With those beliefs of "self" as constant, pleasant, real, and attractive holding sway, we operate with a willingness to avoid investigation of what lies beneath the surface.

Those mistaken beliefs defend and protect our craving for the continued ongoingness of our unexamined sense of self. They leave us ignoring the limitation and lack of ease that is ever present in the universe of self.

If we do notice suffering—in the form of displeasure or craving or disappointment or frustration—we often still look outwardly for its causes and outwardly for its alleviation. Until our minds are well trained in discernment and our mindful attention kept much more constantly in remembrance, we misattribute the causes of our suffering and we misattribute what might lead to its alleviation. We so often try to explain suffering from within the small, distorted perspective of ignorance. We look for the "culprit"—we blame. Contemporary Catholic mystic Richard Rohr reminds us bluntly—but lovingly—"No one else is your problem."

The acknowledgment of the suffering that we experience every day, throughout the day—in the form of tightness and separation and a walled-in sense of self that must be defended—is the beginning realization of the first noble truth. It is more than worth the effort to focus inquiry here, to pay attention to the base-line level of tension in which we live and have lived for decades. This is not to judge ourselves or to despair—that's just "self" adding its two cents again. We focus inquiry into the first noble truth to realize that truth, to see what's so.

What we see is suffering, great and small, gross and subtle. We won't experience liberation until we recognize the tight and binding grip in which self—experienced as utterly separate from grace—holds us.

Many times, it seems, we need just the right amount of suffering to get our attention. Loss, illness, grief, or the discouragement that "self" can place upon our spiritual journey can get our attention. Suffering is grace's "fierce face." It can bring us to our knees. The truth of suffering has always been known to those who either have had the courage to look or those who have choicelessly been brought face to face with suffering. Psalm 130, known as *De Profundis*, echoes all our voices when attention recognizes the truth of suffering, "Out of the depths I have cried to Thee, O Lord."

Let's pause again—just a few minutes for a short, focused look, using the questions below, one by one. The questions point us where to look. It's helpful to stay with each question until you see what's here in your mind now.

In what state of tension is your body? What is your degree of ease?

Is there something you've read or heard or thought in the last few minutes that spun you off into the contraction of this mistaken sense of who you are? Note the tension, note the thoughts and mental images that leave you in less than ease. Then, check: Can you feel the off-balance quality of confusion? Can you feel tightness? Contraction? What does it feel like inside that walled-in sense of egoic self?

Take some time to note the expenditure of energy involved in maintaining whatever walls you believe separate you from others. Take some more time to note the expenditure of energy involved in maintaining whatever walls you believe separate you from the sacred. Note whatever feelings arise along with the believed separation—and bring compassion to them.

Paying attention is the platform for leaving suffering. Note without judgment our egoic attempts at choreography. Simply witness the truth of the situation. The pause allows us to simply note, to simply see.

Rest in clear seeing. Rest in the present and the capacity to see. Note that there is no "I"-illusion in seeing. Rest in the moment without "I." There is great nourishment to be drawn from such moments. These are the moments Thomas Keating, the great teacher of contemporary Centering Prayer, recognized as the moments in which "divine therapy" can do its work.

6

It's Hard to Be a Person

IT'S HARD TO BE A PERSON. We all know that. Rarely, though, do we fully share such a disclosure with each other. We isolate ourselves, believing that the unease we feel is normal or that no one else feels it or that everyone else feels it and they just have better masks. This thinking keeps each of us feeling even more separate, isolated in silent discouragement or shame. We forget that honest self-disclosure keeps us in communion with each other.

We may occasionally look at our loved ones or strangers on the news and, knowing how difficult a life can be when lived within the paltry resources of a mistaken sense of who we are, feel the warm rush of compassion. Less often do we direct that warm rush of compassion toward ourselves.

Generally, especially as contemplative practitioners, we know that life has the predictable sufferings of aging, illness, and death. We know that life has its sorrows. But the realization of the first noble truth goes far beyond those general or even specific admissions of suffering. The realization of this truth—occurring not in the intellect but in the heart—recognizes the pervasiveness of limitation, confusion, and unease in the separate self-sense.

Once we've given voice to the truth, once that truth is utterly realized, the wisdom of the heart sees and knows and opens spontaneously into compassion. It commits to kindness and to compassionate engagement in a world of sorrow, a world of degeneration and corruption and war and violence. It commits to compassionate engagement in a world where greed runs rampant, raping the planet and exploiting the weak. It commits to compassionate engagement, balanced with equanimity, in a world of unexamined, even proudly held, hate.

We recognize that the poor show us what we'd look like without our pretension, the sick what we'd look like without the blessing of health. The powerless show us what we'd look like without our privilege. Although our own mind is the locus of awakening, we are not awakening for ourselves alone. There is no "ourselves alone."

SUFFERING OCCURS in different orders of magnitude in a human life. We may not have yet thoroughly acknowledged the inherent, enduring unease of "being a self." Chances are, though, we *have* acknowledged our suffering before—especially when it's been intense or protracted. By a certain age, we've all known heartbreak, struggle, and profound disappointment.

Humanity knows suffering—the great, acknowledged "vale of tears." Each of us is asked to bear it in this precious life. An insight from the Sufi tradition views our task as human beings as one of transforming suffering into joy. Human suffering is searing and poignant. It can open our hearts and our sense of connection with every other suffering being.

When we look closely, though, we can discern that the sorrows of our humanity are of a different order than the personal tensions and reactivities of our egoic sense of self.

Although it may take many of us a while to acknowledge the pervasive dissatisfaction of the separate self-sense, whatever dissatisfaction we did acknowledge in the past was probably what led us to set out on a spiritual path to begin with. The prolonged unease of living within an "I"-illusion can bring us to a point where we begin to reach out for a peace we've intuited, a peace grace has hinted at, whispered to us about, opened the window upon at times. We go out in search of the comfort of peace.

At the beginning of our spiritual path, we're too enmeshed in ignorance to be seeking anything but a cure or a comfort. We look for comfort in a teaching, in a teacher, in a ritual. We search for something promising more than the egoic self had been able to provide up until that point. We take up a path that can, perhaps for a time, diminish the depression or hopelessness or stress. Our sense of self may feel relieved, assuaged, comforted.

For quite a while on a spiritual path, our goal is to land in a sense of self that feels "easier." We can continue for a while to ignore the truth that suffering is self's constant companion. They arise together. One does not appear without the other.

Many spiritual practices don't consider the foundational necessity of examining this pervasive "given" of self-reference. We really do have to question—over and over—our basic assumption of who we believe ourselves to be, our robotic default position.

Some practices, unskillfully taught or engaged without discernment and wise view, can even strengthen our conviction in the "I"-illusion: "I," the pure and limber yogi, "I," the one directing deeper concentration, "I," the one practicing humility. "I" can find room anywhere if we allow it. In such "I"-filled practice, the very act of engaging in transformative methods—designed to lessen self-clinging and self-cherishing, reducing them to only small wisps of self—can actually strengthen the "I"-illusion.

We need to be willing to surrender whatever self-referential story we're telling—especially in formal practice but certainly also throughout the day. Our surrender allows grace to work its way with us. Such willingness to surrender usually takes time, grace, continued inquiry, and deepening realization. Deepening realization opens us to grace— we offer our being more fully to be transformed by grace. We'll talk about surrender at length later in our discussion.

Let's continue exploring our far-reaching belief in a small, limited understanding of self, a belief that is astonishingly deep and pervasive. Grace has led me to examine this belief, slyly active and always ready to function in my own mind, many times. Once, for example, I woke up abruptly one morning with these words echoing in my mind: "The only thing separating you from grace are all of your beliefs." In that moment, I realized—with an almost physical shock—that my most foundational, oft-repeated belief was the belief that I exist in the way I imagine myself to exist and that that belief pervaded every conception, emotion, perception, action, reaction, and relationship. Buddha compared the consequences of this belief to "tangled reeds." That was my experience—a flash of a vision of how deep-rooted and entangling are self's tentacles—a snarled swirl of hurts and fears and hopes—and how obstructive.

It was a big moment, a moment of real transformative shift. It led me to the helpful habit of labeling all tightness, all minds of turmoil, all self-reference as "ignorance." Using that blanket word to name unease has kept me from tumbling into my ordinary explanations or justifications of the unease. Just labeling the unease as "ignorance" has greatly enabled my practice of surrender. This informal practice drops us out of conceptual mind, the home of self and ignorance, directly into the heart.

IF ASKED TO EXAMINE the basic assumption of self, to inquire into the "I"-illusion, we inevitably run into the self's resistance. When it comes to our own deeply grasped and deeply cherished egoic sense of self, no matter how flawed and inadequate we may judge it to be, no matter how much we feel we long to merge in grace, we're afraid of losing it. Within the universe of self, we're blind to the truth that what does not truly, inherently exist cannot be lost. All we can lose is the suffering that the self we imagine ourselves to be experiences.

I remember once, years ago, driving home after my first encounter with the teachings on the emptiness—the illusoriness—of "self." I balked and sputtered and even mumbled out loud, "Who the hell do they think is driving this car?!" It has taken years of contemplating the teachings to understand that egoic functions drive the car, but egoic functions are not essential identity. Identifying as ego, as illusion, is a dead-end street.

I am not unaware that there is no way to talk about the ultimately illusory nature of the egoic sense of self without using conventional first-person terms such as "I" and "me," even as we're working to disavow ourselves of their ultimate reality. In my phrasing, I have tried to balance conventional usage of all the words in our language that simply assume an inherently existent subjectivity—*I, you, we, us, ourselves,* for example—with the use of the word *attention*. In truth, it is not so much that *we* are trapped and limited in ego—but rather *attention* is trapped.

That distinction is enormous, and recognizing the distinction is liberating. It leads to a newfound freedom. Attention is our holy endowment. It is a quality of formless awareness, of grace, of the sacred. Clear seeing is a skillful use of that precious gift of attention—allowing us, eventually, to discern that the "self" we assume is illusory.

I *do* exist—that's undeniable—but not in the way that I believe. Our participation in grace's display of multiplicity is life's longing for itself, life's love to meet itself. We can have, experience, know, respect, and appreciate our humanity without ego. We can act—with wisdom, love, compassion, and spontaneous, authentic appropriateness—from our humanity without ego.

Our existence offers recognition of a continuum of awareness. We can, as we mature spiritually, come to recognize all frequencies along the continuum. We can recognize the dense, congested, and "gross" frequency of self-reference for what it is. We grow to recognize the "finer" and more subtle frequency of awareness—our essential nature, our *soul* as some traditions call it—as it functions consciously in our individual manifestation. And grace merges attention—that prodigal son—within its profoundly subtle, infinite, and immaculate awareness, sacred in its formless clarity. We can come to freely know and have mobility within self, soul, and spirit.

The "I" or "self" whose tight and binding grip we're working to dislodge here is the egoic sense that believes that, as a fixated, separate and isolated point, it has no access to the rest of the sacred continuum of awareness. We want to "unbind" attention from an illusory sense of our own being, trapped within the confusion of believing itself to be other than grace.

It is ignorance that befogs us and leads us not to question our basic, most habitual assumption of clinging to a self—craving becoming, thirsting for an identity. Ignorance has no resources, no functional capacity, to look beyond itself. It is only grace arising out of compassion with wisdom—the essence of our practice—that allows clear seeing and ever-deepening realization.

The key to piercing the defended boundaries of egoic self is acknowledging the suffering that occurs within those imagined boundaries. That helps us see through and dissolve our illusion that the experience of the separate self-sense is pleasant or one worthy of our attention. The acknowledgment of the truth is clarity without distortion. That clarity without distortion, just like a magnifying glass in the sun, can burn through our perversions of view. It frees our previously trapped attention into awareness beyond self, a fuller experience of the boundaryless continuum of awareness.

Deep, thorough, complete acknowledgment of the suffering inherent in a life experienced only in the narrow, fixated frequency of ego is realization of the first noble truth. It may knock our known world topsy-turvy for a while, but it engenders a previously unimagined expansion of being. It engenders ease. And peace.

THIS MIGHT BE A GOOD TIME to pause a bit for contemplative practice—maybe fifteen or twenty minutes, if you wish. Take some deep breaths and commit to honest, focused inquiry and investigation. It's a pause to inquire into who you think you are, to examine how deep the egoic self-assumption goes.

This pause to examine our self-assumption isn't to look simply at the typical identifications we hold of gender or profession or roles within family and community. It's an opportunity to look at a deeper level. Go through the questions slowly, if you wish, whole-heartedly—with curiosity and compassion. Ask for the blessing of clear seeing. Hold the intention to see from grace.

How do I conceive my "self"? Is the thought that's passing through mine? Does it define me? Am I the thinker of the thought? Am I identifying now as the contemplator of these questions? Are the passing mind-states me?

What *is* my "self"? How pervasive is this self-sense?

What is my experience of living within this self-sense? From what am I separate? How does that separation feel? In my body? In my emotions? In my thoughts?

What is the "I"-illusion in my mind? Is it present now? What is the experience of it in this very moment? What does it veil? Explore, with patience and diligence and specificity, the question: What are the dynamics that lead the sense of "I" to have such a hold on my attention?

What is asking the questions? What is it that's inquiring? What is it that's looking? Can I rest in what is looking? Can I simply rest in awareness, without labels and preconceptions?

And rest for a few minutes in the awareness that is looking. Awareness is, itself, free of content. It is a wonder and a peace.

Rest in its refreshment.

7

The Four Noble Truths

WE CAN RECALL THE FOUR NOBLE TRUTHS. The first truth is suffering exists. The second truth is suffering has causes. The third truth is the cessation of suffering is an untroubled state, available for us all. And the fourth is that there are authentic paths to the cessation of suffering.

Our understanding of the four noble truths holds great benefit if we wish to awaken from the dream of self and suffering. These truths are worthy of frequent recall and contemplation. It is of immeasurable benefit to recognize the truth of them in our own minds. As the realizations become our own, we find ourselves simultaneously grateful and humbled. We're grateful to recognize the truth and humbled that we're simply recognizing the truth that has been true all along.

Suffering exists—that is a given when attention is confined within unmindfulness. The experience of living at the mercy of ignorance is called, in Buddhism, *samsara*. Samsara is not a place but a set of conditions held in orbit by ignorance and characterized by tension, confusion, and the egoic sense of self. I'll use the word *samsara* here to refer to the domain of "self" and suffering.

As we first allow ourselves to open to the truth of suffering, we go through some fairly predictable sequential changes. These changes reflect the level of depth and penetration of our inquiry. Initially, approaching these teachings we find resistance. The "life's not *that* bad," the "I don't want to look at life that way" thoughts; or the "this doesn't really have anything to do with me" thought as if the "me" it doesn't really have anything to do with isn't pervaded with a deep, sad sense of estrangement.

We are all initially, deeply entrenched in and attached to the "I"-illusion. Unmindful, we're quite willing to ignore the suffering inherent within "self" and the degree of distance "self" places between our attention and the grace for which we yearn.

With continued and deepening inquiry into the nature of self and suffering, many simply back away. Many find the inquiry depressing or too demanding, and they discontinue the investigation. As we all know, in our egoic sense of self, comfort is often chosen over truth.

For those who stay the course and continue to inquire into the truth of living under the spell of ignorance and the samsaric suffering it spawns, two things arise with increasingly penetrating power. One is compassion for ourselves and all others. Compassion, deep and authentic, always arises with wisdom. The second thing that arises with continued inquiry is a determined curiosity about the origin of samsara. We seek to understand the dynamics that create suffering so that we might unbind attention from it. Our willingness to apply wise view to the workings of our own minds is worthy of respect. Our pausing and our honest inquiry are meaningful acts. We've begun, hopefully, to see that ignorance—the unwillingness to see—is the fundamental supporting condition of both "self" and the suffering that inevitably co-arises with "self."

Seeing is powerful. It invites in wisdom and a genuine curiosity. Opening the window on the truth of suffering leads us to a commitment, a determined desire to understand the origin of all the unease. We will focus later at length on the causes of suffering as we explore the dynamics of dependent arising. We will learn to recognize the factors of samsara, the system of conditions giving rise to the "I"-illusion in our own minds.

Our growing understanding of the forces within the samsaric system—whatever the depth of our insight, is the beginning realization of the second noble truth, the truth of the origin of suffering. The way out of "self" is through "self." The way out of suffering is to pay attention to the suffering—unmasking its dynamics and the tense, limiting consequences of the dynamics. The recognition of suffering's causes allows us the freedom of option. Option was absent when the underlying dynamics were unexamined—hidden in ignorance and masked by our desirous attachment to the egoic sense of self.

Only discerning wisdom can free attention from entrapment and flexibly recognize options for skillful action. In discerning wisdom, we see what's actually going on. We can begin to employ "skillful means," proven transformative practices. Employing skillful means is the very essence of the fourth noble truth—the truth of the path leading to the cessation of suffering.

We will work with the wisdom of insight, of clear seeing—a seeing so thorough and so penetrating that it pierces the illusion of the "I" who suffers. Wisdom's clear seeing is realization; it is liberative.

Our clear seeing has so much more potency than mindless habituation. As Nisargadatta, the nondual Indian mystic, observed: "The state of witnessing is full of power; there is nothing passive about it." When the ignorance that would ignore the truth of the unexamined human condition ceases, suffering and the self who suffers cease. Nisargadatta noted: "It is in the very nature of a mistake to cease to be when seen."

Renunciation, the willingness to surrender, often arises spontaneously with our realizations. The depth of our willingness to engage in the practice of self-surrender is determined by the depth and stability of our realization. Realization is the blessing of recognizing the essential. With this recognition, this insight, surrender of all that is inessential occurs with greater spontaneity. Insight and surrender are transformative paths—two of the paths to suffering's cessation, to the end of the "I"-illusion.

Authentic transformative practices are the path to awakened mind. They are also the expression of awakened mind—grace working on us and in us and through us. For as long as even a wisp of self remains, a wisp that still considers that it might be separate from grace, it is best to keep that wisp in a cooperative stance vis-à-vis grace. The path, the fourth noble truth, keeps us pointing in the right direction— toward light.

As we proceed on our path, we come to see that grace is with us every step of the way. Our awakening has very little to do with egoic effort beyond requiring our intention to align within grace's work upon us. We do this naturally as we come to recognize grace, grow to trust in it, and come to know that our essential nature is not other than grace.

The peace that we've experienced in the pausing and the insight— the resting in the gaps—led us to at least a tiny realization of the truth of the cessation of suffering. The peace *is* the cessation. The peace is our taste of awakened mind, our taste of freedom. We will recognize the third noble truth as the truth of the cessation of suffering in our own experience. Suffering ceases as attention rests more deeply in truth, as we increasingly surrender attachment to "self."

PAUSE AGAIN, IF YOU WILL. These short bursts of focused inquiry are very helpful. Recollect an experience of acknowledged suffering. Even a fairly benign example will do—an instance of frustration, animosity, anxiety, or discouragement.

How entrenched, even as you recall the experience, was the belief in the self who suffered? Note how intricately woven the sense of self is in this particular story of suffering. We can sense entrapment in the nature of our thoughts, in the sensations of the body, in the openness or "closedness" of our heart.

Note, in your recollection, how the "I"-illusion and the suffering co-arise. As you note the thoughts, the emotions, the sensations that arise within the recollection, watch how fleeting each one is. Simply watch for a few minutes.

Watch for the gaps between the ever-changing appearance and disappearance of all that arises. Finding a gap, rest in it. There is no "I" in the gap. Rest in that peace for a couple of minutes more. That peace will feed and encourage us and light our way home.

EVERY WISDOM TRADITION offers an authentic path, a practice vehicle that can transform our ignorance and unbind us from our limitation in ego. There are many. They are beautiful—humanity's greatest legacy.

In this book, we will work with particular practices—inquiry leading to insight leading to spontaneous surrender. Inquiry is a focused mind, committed to creating the meditative equipoise that *can* see. Insight is the realization seen and known. Surrender is a renunciation of previous attachment and identification, a release of ignorance. With a commitment to seeing the truth of how things are, we follow a path of wise view, of penetrating understanding of the universal causal factors of the separate self-sense. The teachings on dependent arising—as we will explore next—illuminate the attention-trapping web created in the interplay of these causal factors. With wise view, with recognition, the web is unraveled in seeing.

The less we believe in the illusions created within the unconscious conditions of life-in-form—the conditions of dependent arising—the less our attention is trapped within the paradigm they create and within the assumptions and unease of the paradigm. Once we see through the illusion, we no longer assent to it. It's like watching a great magician perform his pièce de résistance. We wow, we marvel; we're stunned with what we believe we see. When the secret is revealed, we can see the illusion as illusion—perhaps still enjoying it but no longer believing it or clinging to it. The distance between enjoying and clinging can be measured in light years.

In the great transformative shift that arises after seeing through illusion, the egoic sense of self—once so defended—becomes available for a joyful surrender. No one needs the burden, the confinement. The truth of the path carries us out of the tight and binding grip of self, out of samsara, and directly to the recognition of grace as our own essential nature. It frees us to know, experience, and abide in the ever-deepening realizations of the vastness of Being.

8

The Conditions of Self

As is so for many of us, I have been the grateful recipient of insights born of centuries—indeed, millennia—of practice within the many wisdom traditions pouring into this time and place, here and now. Among the eighty-four thousand Buddhist teachings, three sets of teachings have had the greatest impact on my life. The contemplation of them and my engagement in practices associated with them have "moved my mind." They've effected deep transformative shifts in both my being and my view. These three teachings with which I so resonate are those we've explored in the four noble truths, the dependent arising teachings we're about to explore, and the teachings of the profound Heart Sutra.

We will continue to look at the teachings on the four noble truths throughout our contemplative exploration in *Unbinding*. They are pivotal understandings. We will look later at the beautiful and paradigm-shattering Heart Sutra and hopefully open ourselves to all it has to say.

For now, let's begin to explore Buddha's insights into dependent arising. They are central to the teachings he offered to guide us to our liberation—our conscious recognition of grace as our essence, our ground. Through our exploration and contemplation, we can mine some of the riches of Buddha's awakened realizations.

The teachings on dependent arising shed light on the dynamics that create an egoic sense of self, a self who suffers. Buddha's insight into conditionality, the interplay of a system of twelve mutually influencing conditions, illuminates our compulsive involvement in self and suffering. His teachings also illuminate how our disenchantment and consequent disengagement from that limiting cycle leads to an increasingly willing and joyful self-surrender.

The dependent arising teachings describe the endless patterned movement that continually creates samsara. In that rutted cycling, the direction is always back into a small and separate sense of self, an eddy in the stream. It is, as we have discussed, a closed paradigm with no hope for the end of suffering within it, in spite of all our maneuvering and wishful thinking.

Our sincere and open inquiry into these processes as they occur in our own experience of living can illuminate the dynamics of how attention gets lost in ignorance. Through our personal investigation of and inquiry into the teachings, we can begin to see through the illusions of our imagining. It can be helpful to think of the teachings of dependent arising as the dynamics that occur as we turn away from the light and cast the huge, obscuring shadow of self across reality.

Dependent arising describes "the system of suffering" that arises in that shadow. It is an organized structure, existing to endure, to maintain its viability. The system of suffering traps attention within it. Can we not recognize how bound in limitation and bewilderment our own attention has been?

Let's inquire into the conditions of self.

MY EMPHASIS IN THIS BOOK is on sharing realizations, insights, and exercises in such a way as to be accessible, practical, and transformational. Through this exploration and contemplation, may we all allow grace to effect transformative shifts in our being, our view, our ways of knowing—here and now.

The dependent arising teachings are profound, complex, and dazzlingly sophisticated. They have been studied and contemplated for more than two and a half thousand years, with many a commentary written about them. Some of the insights in these commentaries have to do with the very closely observed experience of the conditions as they spin our minds with intensity in the present moment. Some have to do with insight into the vast context in which this dependent arising is taking place. They elucidate the implications of the dynamic interplay of causal conditions in a moment, in an hour, over decades, over a lifetime, and back into past lives and on into future lives.

One of my first teachers, Sant Ajaib Singh, taught that we owe each other the truth, that we have an obligation to offer each other only what we know to be true. He taught that, in the midst of such common suffering and confusion, it would be a disservice to do otherwise. His suggestion was to always preface statements we only believe or think with: "This is what I believe" or "This is what I think." Although ideas are often helpful to us, they are of a different order than that which we know. I do not possess the clarity of vision to know anything about past and future lives and so will not discuss them here. Buddha too warned that we not assume too easily that we've penetrated to the depths of these teachings while acknowledging the benefit of exploring and contemplating them.

Although their nuanced precision is stunning, there is much in this body of teachings on dependent arising, including centuries of comments upon Buddha's realized awareness, that did not touch me for a long time. Perhaps this was the "dust" in my eye, but I seemed to get stuck at a conceptual level with them, feeling overwhelmed. At a certain point in my life, a powerful inner force urged me to simplify my spiritual practice, to keep it all simple. The traditional commentaries on dependent arising felt too complicated to be useful to me. I have no desire to be a Buddhist scholar or indeed any kind of scholar at all. I want ever-deepening awakening. Dietrich Bonhoeffer, the Christian theologian and practitioner, gave us all sound advice when he declared he was not as interested in the theology of compassion's definitions as he was in embodying compassion.

My intention to open to the teachings on dependent arising remained, however, and increased. This led to a much simpler formulation of them in my mind than some of the ways in which they are often taught. This formulation rendered them more accessible to me and revealed some ways to engage in practice with them that felt authentic and illuminating. It is this simpler, more practical formulation that I share in *Unbinding*.

Over time I've come to see that our experiential realization of these teachings depends upon three things. The first has to do with contemplation—clear seeing. Our deep penetration of the workings of these mutually influencing conditions, both in our own long-term and momentary experience of life, leads to realization. Although our tendency is to continue to try to find fulfillment within those conditions, in reality, we recognize that we are playing a losing game.

The second has to do with self-surrender—our willingness to let go of our entrapment in an endless cycle that holds no lasting promise of peace or awakening. Surrender involves more than simply the willingness to let go of any thought that's been tugging at us, for example— although it certainly includes that. Surrender has to do with releasing our attachment to and identification with thought, with the mind's wanderings in general, except as conceptuality and mental operations serve a useful, practical, additive function. Surrender is the emptying of the mind—the emptying of its beliefs and fabrications, especially the fabrication of the "I"-illusion.

Most of the thousands of thoughts flying through our minds each day have no value. Most are mistaken, based in ignorance. Unmindful, they are in service to the paradigm of self. The willingness to surrender them arises from discernment as to which have benefit and which do not as well as from disenchantment with the illusions ignorance creates. The willingness to surrender operates in service to awakening.

The third factor upon which our realizations depend is grace. Our realizations deepen with the intensity with which grace arises in us, the openness we have to making room for it through self-surrender, and the transformational practices of contemplation and meditation.

All three—contemplation, surrender, and grace—condition each other in ways that lead toward conscious communion in the sacred nature of reality. All three bring the insights of the teachings to our heart's understanding.

WE'LL APPROACH THE TEACHINGS on dependent arising together in a language and a presentation that is, hopefully, understandable and useful to practitioners within any tradition. Their contemplation leads, ultimately, to the self-surrender to which we as mystics aspire. This self-surrender liberates us from our fixated point on a vast continuum of awareness, a stream of frequencies wide and endless.

Buddha's insights on dependent arising were his core realizations upon awakening. This was his view from clear seeing—from the cleansing of his perception and conception. They arose from immaculate awareness. When we explore and contemplate these insights, when we inquire into what's actually going on, we afford ourselves the opportunity to also engage in a deep and welcome cleansing.

Clear seeing allows deep cleansing. It removes the dust from our eyes—wiping away the cobwebs of our ignorance and dissolving the sense of self ignorance continually gives birth to. Unlike wisdom, self has no peepholes into reality. None whatsoever.

Insight into this system of suffering allows us to understand the formation of the wall that keeps us within limitation. We can, with contemplation and inquiry, begin to see how the walls of the separate self-sense arise and begin to watch ignorance wreak its havoc within those walls. Likewise, with contemplation and inquiry, we can begin to note the conditions that have convinced us and sustained the deceptive conviction that the knot of self, the "I"-illusion, has substance, has reality, is true.

Buddha listed twelve mutually influencing conditions in his exposition of dependent arising, the tendencies and dynamics that operate unseen in the fog of ignorance. All of the conditions set the climate for each of the others, and all are co-arising, mutually affecting, everoscillating. Their dynamics are a universal map of suffering, a diagram of the causes and conditions creating samsara.

Ignorance is the fundamental condition giving rise to the tension of the self we presume. Of great influence in the interplay is another of the conditions—becoming, the desire to have the entire self-creating cycle continue. Other conditions include karmic formations, consciousness, name-and-form, sensory apparatus, contact, feeling, craving, grasping, birth, aging-and-death (suffering). We'll explore each one in some depth.

We want to understand these impersonal patterns or conditions as they operate in us since we experience the suffering they produce as directly personal. We feel the suffering; we know the experience; we get lost in its confusions and unease. Buddha's shared insight about the dynamics of dependent arising calls us to see how we participate in the patterned cycling. It calls us to recognize that the suffering we experience is not something that's done to us. An understanding of dependent arising reveals that there is no one to blame—not even "me."

As individual manifestations of grace, though, we are responsible, if we wish, to end the experience of limitation and stress through cooperative agency with grace. We want to untangle our confusion and the misrepresentations these patterns create so that we may unbind and freely function as manifestations and offerings of grace in a world begging for mercy.

THE TWELVE CONDITIONS of dependent arising are the players on the "system of suffering" team. Let's begin with some very simple definitions of each of them.

Ignorance in this context is the confused fog that arises from our unwillingness to actually inquire into the truth. It rests on assumptions and mistaken conclusions. The root of ignorance is resistance to seeing things as they are, a willingness to ignore. Living within the condition of ignorance could be compared to following a compass that, unbeknownst to us because we haven't bothered to check, stubbornly avoids pointing true north.

Karmic formations refers to the condition of habit, deeply ingrained. Thoughts and other conditioned reactivities pass over these karmic formations and are conditioned by them, in much the same way as ocean currents are conditioned by the topography of mountains and valleys on the ocean floor, conditioned even by rippled patterns in the sand. Here are our stories, our assumptions, our desires, our beliefs, our narrative-consistent memories. They give shape to momentary arisings.

Consciousness is the sense-making function, the cohering function. It is an *enactive* function. It fills in the "gaps" and inconsistencies ignorance prefers to ignore and often views as chaotic and/or threatening. Intent upon weaving a seamless narrative, the condition of consciousness jumps over careful contemplation, jumps to quick conclusions. It can be recognized in our aversion to chaos, our passion for instant gratification, and our constant need to feel we've established terra firma, no matter how illusory.

Name-and-form refers to the condition that labels and brings into form via labeling. These are our fabrications. Based on the memories of karmic formations, name-and-form functions to pull appearances out of potentiality and into the foreground of attention. This condition functions to form both the egoic self and the world we experience within self-reference.

The six senses—sometimes called *sensory apparatus*—is the condition that allows form to be seen, sound to be heard, odor to be smelled, taste to be tasted, touch to be felt, and thoughts to be registered. This condition is the "equipment" of manifesting in human form—the eyes, the ears, the nose, the mouth, the sensory capacity of the body, and the capacity of conceptual mind.

Contact is the condition that arises when form is seen, sound is heard, odor smelled, taste tasted, touch felt, and thoughts registered. It is the moment of connection between that which apprehends and the object of apprehension.

Feeling is the condition of reaction to contact, itself conditioned by the other conditions. Feeling upon contact arises automatically as either positive, negative, or neutral. The latter feeling, neutral, is sometimes referred to as neither-positive-nor-negative. Every single moment of contact has an accompanying feeling.

Craving is a condition that arises with a personalization of feeling. There is an ingrained inclination, a psychic orientation, to act upon or lean into—with a slight sense of identification or ownership—whatever feeling arises.

Grasping is a condition of irresistible desire. It functions as a compulsive urge operating within the interplay of the other conditions of dependent origination. It doesn't matter if it's the urge to slam on the brake as a truck is about to crash into us or the urge to scratch an itch on our cheek. Regardless of what the urge is for, it is held as necessary for survival. It operates, although this is not necessarily articulated, as if whatever the urge is about is a life or death issue. The urge to grasp arises and attention blindly follows.

Becoming is the condition that defines the blind follower of the grasping. This is the condition that gives rise to the need to be the self slamming on the brakes, the need to be the self scratching the itch. Becoming refers to our hunger for existence, our desire to maintain an ego, our thirst for a sense of being somebody. This is our need to have a place to stick the nametag. The condition of becoming is experienced as a necessity, a given, and a hoped-for refuge.

Birth is the apparent arising of the blind follower. It arises in dependence upon becoming's need to be the blind follower. Birth is the outcome of the issues preceding and mutually conditioning it. It is the birth of the experience of a temporary satiation and a "self," the experiencer of the satiation.

Aging-and-death is the condition birth gives rise to, whether this occurs in the perceived time span of the physical body or in the flash of a momentary spin of the cycle of the mutually influential conditions of dependent arising.

Although the urge for a self is present, you will note that *self*—"I" or "me" or "mine"—is *not* present as one of the twelve conditions in this system of suffering. It is not mentioned—nowhere to be seen.

IN THE NEXT CHAPTER we will examine how "self" arises and forms as a consequence of these conditioning factors—how the "I"-illusion is endlessly given rise to within the dynamics of their system. The greatest benefit for each of us will come from recognizing this arising and forming within our own minds. Recognizing is literally re-cognizing—it changes our understanding; it changes our view. It is one of the ways in which we unbind.

9

What's Going on Here?

STRESS AND UNEASE arise for most practitioners with some frequency throughout each day. Perhaps I'm moving in the wrong circles, but I do not know many people for whom this does not hold some truth—myself included.

Samsara's quality of tension—a product of conditioning and conditioned dynamics, all impersonal—should remind us to look closely at what is happening beneath the surface of appearances and assumptions. Stress and unease can serve as red flags, indicating that something other than peace, something other than equanimity, is shaping the experience of the moment. We can recognize any level of dissatisfaction as an indication that our attention is trapped in ignorance, that ignorance is operating and churning out illusions.

It is helpful to train ourselves to remember that when stress and unease arise, *curiosity* is one of our most beneficial responses. The kindest, wisest thing we can do for ourselves is ask, what's really going on here?

Buddhist teacher Martine Batchelor, following Zen tradition, describes the impact of this approach: "Great questioning, great awakening; small questioning, small awakening; no questioning, no awakening."

Our willingness to see the hidden dynamics that have run our lives—up close and personal—can pop us out of entrapment in endless, mindless circularity. It can release the eddy into the stream. Inquiry allows attention's leap into a more sane and spacious continuum of awareness. Inquiry, the willingness to see—a willingness that can grow into an eagerness to see—brings us into the truth of the present moment.

The American philosopher/practitioner Ken Wilber refers to an act such as radical *willingness to see* as the addition of creativity to karma. Inquiry is a creative act in that it introduces a new factor to the conditioned system. It disrupts the "cogs." During moments of inquiry, the function of the system cannot proceed as it typically does—unconsciously—and, therefore, cannot continue surreptitiously churning out self and suffering. Inquiry is a creative act in that it allows the birth of wisdom—an utterly new perspective, stance, and refuge.

Such creativity, capable of altering the direction of blind karmic habits, is evidence of grace's evolutionary impetus toward ever-deepening realizations. That addition of the practice of inquiry into relentless karmic patterning can free attention from its habituated orbit just as an electron, with a quick infusion of energy, can break free from an atom. Wisdom—clear seeing—provides the energy to make the quantum leap.

When we see through the illusion of who we thought we were, wisdom burns away our false beliefs and mistaken hopes in the illusory refuge of self. As wisdom burns through all the conceptual scaffolding, attention can land straight in the bodily seat of wisdom and compassion at the level of the heart. Eleventh-century mystic Hildegard von Bingen noted: "An interpreted world is not home." The heart is home; it is true refuge.

Refuge has a beautiful and precise meaning in Buddhism. "Going for refuge" is an action of the whole being. It is based on our willingness to cooperate with grace as it calls our attention home. It is a form of renunciation, of surrender. Letting go of all thoughts of self-reference, we place our entire being in the refuge of awakened mind—grace. We dissolve ordinary conceptual thoughts in acknowledgment of the truth. We cede every inclination to follow any longing other than the longing to follow the path to the truth. We rest in the interconnection of all beings within that truth, within grace.

With growing wisdom we come to recognize without a doubt that the cycle of suffering is allowed and determined in conceptual mind. Conceptual mind has its beneficial uses, certainly. These beneficial uses arise when the powerful function of conceptual mind is employed deliberately, openly, and mindfully. Such a use of conceptuality's function is comparable to a controlled burn, deliberately and with thoughtful informed consideration, undertaken in service to a beneficial ecological purpose.

When conceptual mind is allowed to operate unconsciously, without mindful attention, it allows the conditions of dependent arising to proceed and proliferate. The ensuing cycle produces the complex, mistaken mental mirage of a separate self, inherently existing and prone to suffering. This is comparable to a wildfire that consumes everything in its path.

The conditions of awakening arise through grace at the level of the heart—the seat of knowing, the seat of grace's embodiment in our humanity. With wisdom, with grace, as D. H. Lawrence put it, "the fierce curve of our lives" moves to the depths, "out of sight, in the deep living heart." Wisdom, grace's compassionate gift within our being, allows the seeing that can release our attention and shoot us out of samsara's suffering orbit.

RADICAL RESPONSIBILITY for our own suffering—seeing it, owning it, releasing our attention from identification with ego—is a sign of our maturing depth as practitioners. Such responsibility or accountability—there can be no hint of "blame" here—rests upon a clear recognition. We will explore and inquire into a patterned system of suffering with endlessly spinning conditions that automatically churn out a distorted sense of self with accompanying unease. We need to see it in our own minds. Our growing recognition of the origin of suffering is our growing realization of the second noble truth.

The desire for unbinding, the desire for freedom and simple sanity, arises when we clearly see the cyclic patterns' capacity as the creator of illusions—the fabricated illusions of our self-image as well as all the fabricated, dualistic mental and perceptual images of the world—all we hold as "other." We can grow in our capacity to discern the difference between the not-here, not-now of fabrications and the grounded truth of the present.

When we see the images as illusions, the images no longer fascinate. Their seductive power diminishes. We know mirage as mirage. We become disenchanted. We renounce our attachment to the system. Surrender is renunciation, an aspect of the fourth noble truth, the truth of the path. It sets us free into the lived experience of the third noble truth, the truth of the cessation of suffering.

Understanding the conditioned—knowing its workings and dynamics, knowing our egoic self to be simply an utterly conditioned arising—is a path to the unconditioned. It's a gate. The old adage, "Anyone who knows he is a fool is not such a great fool," has been around a while for a reason.

BECOMING ATTENTIVE to what's actually going on is itself awakening. And what's actually going on in samsaric consciousness is a perpetual, spinning proliferation of ignorance, frivolous indulgence, and unseen robotic habits leading to suffering. This suffering is not simply isolated moments of pain and despair or the predictable sufferings of aging, illness, and death. We're looking at the underlying suffering self experiences each and every moment in its various reactive stances.

Seeing this suffering—the first noble truth—is the first step in cultivating compassion for ourselves and for a suffering world, a world saturated in, permeated by, the universal egoic capacity for destructive hate and exploitive greed. It is, in every significant and meaningful sense, our responsibility to awaken and offer awakened presence.

A million voices have sung some version of these words, "Let there be peace on earth and let it begin with me." Our contemplation of these teachings can allow the realization of that wish.

As we begin to inquire into and clearly see the system of suffering in our own minds, we can come to see, as Buddha did, that all of the conditions of existence as life-in-form—ignorance, karmic formations, consciousness, name-and-form, sensory apparatus, contact, feeling, craving, grasping, becoming, birth, aging-and-death (or suffering)—set the climate for all the others. It is a closed system with multiple, dynamic, unconscious feedback loops.

Again, please note, "self" is not one of the conditions listed above. It is a complex mental and emotional overtone, fed in every moment by the conditions of dependent arising and oblivious to its own tenuousness. "Self" arises as an overtone or byproduct of this spinning cycle. It is a "seed," a latency, produced by past conditions and nurtured by present conditions, setting the stage for continued future appearances of the "I"-illusion.

The illusion of self only holds a grip on us when we're not paying attention to what's actually going on. When we look to find "I" in this spinning, there is no "I" to be found. Without such focused inquiry, we assent to the illusion of an enduring egoic sense of self. Without such focused inquiry, we live our lives within the assumption that somehow there is a *someone* in here—"me"—and that pleasure and even permanent happiness can be found within the spinning conditions. Without such focused inquiry, we do not recognize the system of suffering for what it is.

To see the truth of the patterning that gives rise to the sense of self frees us from the momentum of its spinning web. This liberation is not just a moment-by-moment liberation but a lessening of future manifestations of a blindly grasped, suffering self.

Not one of the conditions is part of our identity—as we typically assume with a casual application of "I" or "me." Nor is any of the conditions a possession of ours—as we typically assume with a casual application of "mine." Each is simply an impersonal arising in a complex interplay of causes.

AS OUR REALIZATION of the second noble truth deepens and stabilizes, we begin to clearly see that suffering has an origin. As our capacity for insight develops and as grace further endows that capacity, we can isolate and identify the causes of suffering.

To look at the conditions of dependent arising is like having a notorious gang gathered in an interrogation room, the naked light shining brightly upon the members. These are the suspects. These are the gang members that have been creating havoc with our lives for decades. Disorderly conduct. Disturbing the peace. Inciting hatred.

Greed and corruption. Fraud. Lying, slander, frivolous accusations. Manipulation and intimidation. We can put the whole lot in a lineup and examine them one by one, remembering all the while that a gang has synergy—its sum is more than the total of its parts. Here, we discover, is the origin of suffering, the causes arrayed before us, available for our understanding.

The traditional teachings on dependent arising tend to be presented in linear order—as links. As we explore the conditions—and their dynamics—we will come to observe the whole spinning cycle more clearly, as it operates in each of our own minds. It is not simply that one condition is influenced by the condition preceding it and then affects the condition following it in linear order—as in a chain or a vertical stack of bricks. It is that, in some senses, but it is more.

Most often, the links are depicted as links in a chain. It is that too, in some senses, but it is more. Perhaps a more helpful way to get a beginning sense of the interplay of the conditions is to think of the pilings, the beams, cables, nuts, and screws, the metals and concrete, the angles and tension that, interacting with each other, create a phenomenon we call a bridge. Once in place each condition conditions and is conditioned by all others. They are mutually dependent. The bridge arises within their mutual dependence.

When you begin to investigate the movements of your own mind, you will see that rather than simply proceeding in an orderly chain of events—like dominoes toppling—the system of suffering occurs in dizzying spurts of energized agenda, fueled by habit and desire and allowed within ignorance. Attention becomes bound within it— trapped inside, with immense gravitational force. The consequence is that who we think we are suffers.

We will get a chance to explore each condition in more depth. We want to take each one as an object of contemplation so that we see it clearly, to see it as "not self," and to see its effects in our own experience. In this way, clearly seeing, we can disidentify from each condition and develop dispassion for it. In contemplation, we will take the opportunity to observe the interplay of the conditions as their dynamics arise in our own minds.

The illusions of hoping for satisfaction, imagining we can permanently secure happiness, and believing that ego is who we are can be dissipated, as mist dissipates in sunlight. What's revealed, in Catholic mystic Martin Laird's beautiful words, is their "sunlit absence."

It seems to me that the various conditioning factors of dependent arising, the conditions giving rise to a limited self-sense and the suffering that limited self-sense experiences, have slightly different functions. This is what has become apparent to me. As we continue to engage in inquiry together, you can begin to see the dynamics of these forces for yourself.

Some conditions hide and obscure—ignorance and consciousness, as we shall see, function as *obscuring* forces. They remove us from the reality of the present moment. Some conditions—name-and-form and craving—create; they function as *creating* forces. They function particularly to bring "self" and form into being.

Some conditions in the pattern of dependent arising determine the nature of the creation brought into being. Karmic formations and feeling are *determining* forces, functioning much as the act of observation in a quantum physics experiment determines whether energy appears as wave or particle.

Our sensory apparatus and the experience of contact exist as *existential* forces—they come with the territory of human experience. These conditions are grounded in our physical existence.

Some conditions are *proliferating* forces. Grasping and becoming keep pushing the entire cycle into continued cycling. They proliferate its unconscious momentum just as a snowball rolling down a hill gains momentum. They are the factors that propel and amplify the rotations of the wheel of conditions creating self and suffering. Picture a croupier giving an extra spin to the roulette wheel.

Some conditions—birth and aging-and-death—are *imprinting* forces, deepening the very groove of the cycle's habituation. They endlessly promise hope and endlessly fail to deliver. All the while, they etch their rut ever more deeply, imprinting a familiar tendency toward "self," a familiar incline for future arisings to follow, just as an arroyo in the desert channels the waters of a quick storm.

WE WILL EXPLORE, in just a bit, each of the conditions more extensively in the material ahead. We want to be able to observe the operations of the "wheel of suffering" in our own minds. We will see the illusion-creation of the entire cycle. The wheel of suffering creating the "I"-illusion revolves around a belief in ego as the owner, the agent, the victim, and the only relevant referent. It is blind to the fact that ego is a byproduct of the circling conditions creating it.

We can commit to end our blindness and take heart in the encouragement of Nisargadatta, who counsels: "To see the universe as it is, you must step beyond the net. It is not hard to do so for the net is full of holes."

10

Keys to the Kingdom

WE WILL BE FOCUSING on each of the conditions of dependent arising, one by one—learning to recognize each of them as together they spin their web and their illusions. Before we do, though, it is helpful for each of us to spend some contemplative time—time in meditation—cultivating a strong and heart-felt intention to recognize them, to see through them.

Our own insight into the first noble truth—a recognition that the separate sense of self and a pervasive sense of unease inevitably arise together—and the implications of that insight for each of us can serve as motivation to investigate.

Although there are twelve conditions mutually influencing each other, our liberation from the entire system of suffering does not necessarily depend upon seeing through each of the conditions separately and thoroughly. When we have insight into the second noble truth, we begin to recognize each and every insubstantial and impersonal condition we're exploring as a cause of "personal" suffering. Seeing through one condition is enough to liberate us from the entire system.

Seeing "just enough" allows us to discontinue our investment in the continuing cycle. It allows us to become dispassionate, disenchanted.

When we can look through a "link" of dependent arising with dispassion, we have already renounced our desire to continue in an endless cycle of temporary and illusory gratification. We can, with joy, begin to surrender our habituated clinging to a "self."

Any of the conditions, once seen through, can no longer deceive us. There is an old Buddhist teaching story about a monk who walks into a room and sees a snake. Instantly, he is filled with fear and an intense aversion. Upon investigation, though, the "snake" is revealed to be simply a coiled rope. In that moment of seeing, the "snake," the fear, and the aversion are instantly dispelled. The illusion is unmasked. This is the power of inquiry and insight. When we shine a light the darkness instantly disappears.

Once we remove the power of the condition we're investigating and inquiring into, the other conditions that depend upon the condition we've seen through can no longer arise with the same power. Because the system is one of multiple feedback loops and interdependent conditionality, the entire system collapses when one of the conditions no longer has any power to deceive us. This would be analogous to removing a stone from the arc of a stone archway. The archway collapses. No matter how substantial it had seemed, no matter how long it had endured, the archway is no longer an archway.

So, as we enter our exploration of each of the conditions of dependent arising, we commit to seeing with intention and with committed focus, inviting and allowing the open eyes of ever-present and ever-cooperative grace. These are the keys that can shut down the entire system of self and suffering. These are the keys that can simply turn it off. When we investigate the conditions of dependent arising—with mindful attention and intention—we grow to recognize them as keys that can stop the endless cycling. In so doing, we are practicing the fourth noble truth—the path to the cessation of suffering.

There is a story—it may be apocryphal but it is lovely and illustrative—that gives a sense of the level of committed focus necessary to clearly see.

In the Boston music scene at the time of Keith Jarrett's stunning masterpiece, the Köln Concert, there was a tale going around about the development of his virtuosity. It was said that he had a Russian piano teacher who trained him with great precision and powerful discipline. She trained him in a path to mastery. She asked him, it was said, to spend eight hours each day playing one note on the piano—one note only—every day for a week. She asked him to dedicate himself to knowing each of the notes intimately. He spent eighty-eight weeks, the story goes, doing just that.

He came to intimately know eighty-eight keys. We only have twelve conditions to work with in the system of dependent arising. Clearly seeing—knowing—any one of the conditions is a key to turn off the whole incessantly buzzing, illusion-creating, harmonic-producing system. Once we have become even vaguely aware of the behind-the-scenes machinations of samsara, we recognize that it's always been a creator of distortion and a destroyer of ease. Our healthy desire to see the compositional factors of our suffering increases.

We have twelve "keys" to explore. It is wise to devote a measure of time to examining, investigating, and recognizing each one of them. No need, necessarily, to spend eight hours a day on each one for a week. Our task is simpler than Keith Jarrett's development of his musical talent. We simply need to see "just enough." We do this when we deliberately, in mystic poet Rainer Maria Rilke's words, "live the question."

I INVITE YOU to make a commitment to yourself, if you wish, that you will spend a certain amount of time examining each of the twelve conditions, both in formal meditation and throughout the moments of your days. It is important when we make a commitment to this that we only make a commitment we know that we can keep. The mind is very literal. If we set a precedent in our minds that our "word"—our conscious commitment—means nothing, the habituated machinations are only too happy to oblige. They *want* to continue unimpeded.

So, whether you decide to devote a day to the contemplation and exploration of each condition as it operates in your own mind or an hour or ten minutes, make sure it is a commitment you keep. And respect yourself for the commitment. Any looking, any seeing, is better than none at all. A. H. Almaas, the mystic teacher of the Diamond Approach, points out to us that "to contact the deeper truth of who we are, we must engage in some activity or practice that questions what we assume to be true." The path of inquiry, marked by innocence and curiosity, is a noble path. It is appropriate to humbly and gratefully respect the dignity of our longing and intention to see.

A refrain in this book, one that can encourage each of us every time we repeat it, comes from Tibetan Buddhist teachings. The refrain is this: "Recognition is liberation." That liberation is the third noble truth—the cessation of suffering, alighting in unbinding.

PART THREE

Setting the Stage

11

Ignorance

BUDDHA, in speaking of his insight into dependent arising, simply and elegantly noted, "Such is the origination of the entire mass of suffering."

The twelve conditions of dependent arising, often called "links" to note their mutually conditioning interplay, are held together by ignorance and craving. Ignorance and craving, along with the other conditions, create both the egoic self-sense and the world "self" experiences. What holds the sequencing of links together as quick energetic spurts is our agenda, our wish to have it continue. Ignorance obligingly looks the other way.

The cycle of suffering, the dependent arising of suffering, is generally taught with a recognition of ignorance as one of its most powerful engines. Ignorance is pervasive—the fundamental condition giving rise to samsara. It fuels the circle of obscuration that leaves us feeling small and alone, eddies in a stream.

Ignorance is not only unwilling, it is incapable of seeing beyond the conditioning. It can never know the unconditioned, the Absolute we long to recognize and with which we yearn for conscious communion. It sets the stage for a sense of subjectivity to arise and obscure the ever-presence of grace.

For us to mistakenly assume ourselves as separate and inherently existing, ignorance needs to be in place—up and running as a conditioning factor. This is the case in all of the unmindful moments of our lives. Ignorance places a defended barrier between grace and the immeasurable potential of our precious human life—a potential ignorance holds hostage. It traps attention, blocking its entry into greater depth and more subtle awareness. It keeps us at survival, in samsara, in "self."

Buddha's view is that ignorance is the absence of knowledge and vision of things as they are. *Ignorance* is not a bully's playground taunt, but a technical term with specific meaning.

Avidyā is the Sanskrit word for ignorance. Avidyā's literal translation is "not paying attention" or "absence of attention." Ignorance is a constriction of attention. It is a great collapse of grace's vast and formless awareness, never absent yet utterly missed and unnoticed—even resisted—by that ignorance. Ignorance is the condition that allows mistaken beliefs and assumptions to continue fabricating their conclusions behind the fog ignorance spreads. It is a breeding ground for illusion.

Ignorance hides the dynamics of the very formation of the "I"-illusion. In this way, we can see it as the basis of all delusions. It is the basis of our most fundamental mistake in the way we hold ourselves, the world, and the objects in the world as "real." Ignorance validates and assents to whatever beliefs we endow with our capacity to believe—especially our belief in the substantive reality of the egoic self-sense. It gives our unexamined beliefs a free pass.

Our willingness to explore the operation of ignorance in our own minds will assist in undermining our mistaken, distorting assumptions about reality. Without looking we are not even aware of all of our assumptions. When we clearly and piercingly see through the condition of ignorance—whether suddenly or gradually—ignorance melts. As the force of ignorance dissipates, our mistaken assumptions lose their supporting condition. They are seen as deceptive—like the moment we recognize a con man in action. We can no longer be deceived.

No longer deceived, we will still live in the world of "conventional reality." Tibetan Buddhists refer to conventional reality with a phrase that translates literally as "all-false reality." We will live in that consensual reality with all the laws of form—where else would we live these human lives? But, with the dispelling of ignorance, our attention and identity can be freed from all our binding misconceptions. The great Zen teacher Shunryu Suzuki was once asked, "How much ego do we need?" His reply was simple: "Just enough so you don't step in front of a bus." We learn to live lightly, without the heaviness of a "self" weighted with belief and assent.

We can, with wisdom, reorient ourselves to the soul interior to the "self," to the light behind all the appearances, to the grace manifesting the entire display. Wisdom allows us to freely engage our humanity without being duped by it.

When we recognize appearances as appearances, without the belief that anything—including the self—exists in the way we have believed it to exist, suffering is diminished. Although there may be hard punches to the ego and dark nights of the soul as we merge ever more deeply with truth, suffering—both that which we experience and that which we inflict—decreases. This has the truth of an axiom, once we recognize this for ourselves. The closer we are to truth, the less suffering we experience.

With this realization and this merging into grace, we can begin to embody the third noble truth—the truth of the cessation of suffering—and become an offering to the world. This is the purpose of a human life, to realize our essential nature, to know and be love. Thomas Keating, along with every other ripened spiritual practitioner, reminds us, "Divine love has to be manifested as well as experienced." Our witness and our offering signal the ripening of the path.

IGNORANCE FUNCTIONS as the ground environment, setting the climate for all the other conditions of dependent arising to run freely. In the absence of wisdom, they run automatically, without monitoring and without beneficial purpose, in service only to a desire-driven cycling. When we talk about *ground environment*, we can think of a toxic work environment, for example, and how it can set the uneasy and reactive tone for our thoughts, feelings, and actions throughout the workday. The ground environment of ignorance sets the stage for suffering.

Ignorance is deeply ingrained. Without mindful attention, ignorance is a given, a certainty. It sets the incline for all the other conditions to slide along on and tilts the scales in craving's favor. Ignorance turns away from all that might slow or erode or block our compulsion to continue to grasp and crave. This turning away has an energetic force that functions to spin the wheel of suffering, to give it another push, increasing its momentum.

Ignorance sustains the unexamined, unsupported delusion of hoping fulfillment might still be ours within the spinning cycle. Ignorance does not recognize that the illusions it inextricably has a hand in creating are, in fact, illusions. Ignorance does not discern that illusions cannot quench craving.

We all know the lists, the *if-onlys,* the *whens*: when I go to college, if only I had a job, when I get married, if only I had or didn't have children, when the kids go to college, when I get divorced, if only I had enough money, when I retire, etc. Although happiness has never appeared before in any stable or enduring way, we harbor the recurring, unreflective thought that when our desired conditions are met, *then happiness will be lastingly mine.* Such is our ignorance talking. Its script is handed to it by craving. We can see the endless cycling, the entrapment, the binding.

Within ignorance, the tendency is to wish to continue the unexamined cycle, like a hapless hamster spinning a wheel. We remain unaware of how stressful it is to keep an illusion going, to be constantly juggling, to be treading water in a tank. Again: the condition of ignorance is an obscuring force. It hides the truth of what is actually so and it blocks our recognition of ever-present grace.

Ignorance, the "first link" in the system of suffering, functions in a habitually specific way. Its dynamic is one of a stubborn refusal to see. We have all noted this resistance to seeing at times, maybe even in the course of this exploration. Like the velvet ropes in an exhibition hall, ignorance aims to prevent any poking behind the curtain to witness the machinations producing the "I"-illusion. We can think of the scared, lonely man, beating his drums and choreographing the light display, creating the illusion of the Wizard of Oz. Any illusion, let's recall, ceases its enchantment in a single moment of seeing.

Ignorance resists pausing to consider—pausing to investigate—what's actually so. Such investigation would halt the onward rush promising fulfillment.

Ignorance is the condition of turning away from all that we might find uncomfortable, like a toddler covering her ears to what she doesn't want to hear. Ironically, it is most often so that where we turn away is precisely where it might be worthwhile and beneficial to look. We would each benefit from noting in our own minds *where* our resistance arises and *to what*. What do I not want to know? This very not-wanting-to-know is ignorance in action. In *Gone with the Wind*, Scarlett O'Hara speaks for ignorance everywhere when she says, "I don't want to think about it today. I'll think about it tomorrow." Can we recognize our own habitual patterns here?

Ignorance's resistance to looking makes ignorance hard to see, but grace's wisdom is ever present and always available to cooperate once our intention is determined to see. It is kind and wise—skillful—to cultivate that intention and the courage that seeing demands.

Ignorance is conditioned by a yearning for comfort. We'll see this yearning for comfort in all the conditions. This is how craving conditions ignorance and all the other links in mutually influential dynamics. In many ways it could be said that ignorance operates in service to craving. It engenders busyness and mind-numbing addictions—both subtle and profound—and every other form of obscuration. It spawns small talk, meaningless talk—inner and outer, filling (or killing) our time, frivolously wasting precious moments of this finite life.

We can ask, how pervasive is my wish for comfort? To what level of pettiness does it reach? Have we so "refined our taste" that less and less appears as comfort? Let's never forget that even asking these questions is a sign of the privilege of our fortunate circumstances in a world of so much misery. So many billions—that's with a "b"—live their whole lives with few of the comforts we take utterly for granted.

Ignorance operates with a confirmation bias. This manifests as our preference to surround beliefs with agreement and as the habit of interpreting information in such a way as to sustain ignorance's paradigm. None of us needs to look far in our partisan culture to see this tendency in ourselves. We like agreement.

For as long as ignorance functions, that is to say, for as long as we remain without mindful attention, ignorance will attempt to ensure that the self we cherish and cling to will remain unchallenged. While ignorance functions, although we may wish to rearrange our inner and outer circumstances so that life becomes more comfortable, we don't truly want to change the direction, the priorities, and the identifications of our lives. A *New Yorker* cartoon I once saw depicts a group of spiritual aspirants gathered hopefully around a teacher. The caption: "We're hoping you'll lead us on a journey of transformation without requiring any real change."

Ignorance blocks our recognition of the first noble truth—the truth of suffering, the truth that "self" and suffering inevitably arise together. Once that truth is recognized, the longing to surrender the entire samsaric system arises with sincerity and authenticity.

There is something to the condition of ignorance that seems to not want to rock the boat. There is a passivity to ignorance—a conservative wish to maintain the status quo. But, within that passivity, its force can be defensive and aggressive—as if determined to keep us lost and wandering in samsara. Ignorance has succeeded in its function when, after a glimpse of the truth or an inrush of contradictory evidence, it can report back to the rest of the system: "Paradigm unshattered. Mission accomplished."

We can ask ourselves, where do I close down? What do I keep my mind or my heart locked against? What do I not want to see? What am I defending?

One of the best illustrations of ignorance comes to us from ninth-century Catholic mystic Teresa of Avila. In her realizations, she recognized that a powerful indication of the presence of ignorance is "praying as if God were not present." "Praying as if God were not present" is the confused belief in a "self" existing separate from its own essential nature, from all others, and from the sacred. To name ignorance as ignorance within our own minds is to acknowledge that ignorance does not know—and cannot know—the truth. Ignorance keeps attention at a far remove from reality.

Ignorance, in fact, refers to every moment that attention is *not* consciously abiding in grace. It sustains an experience of life that feels a bit like the biblical sense of "cast from Eden." Through the lens of wise view, though, we can see this experience of being cast from Eden—separate from grace—not as punishment but as predicament.

Our growing understanding of the four noble truths illuminates this predicament. The reality of the predicament is the first noble truth—the truth of suffering. As we grow in insight into the dynamics of life-in-form, the dynamics of dependent arising, we realize the second noble truth—the origin of suffering. We can see and recognize the sources of tension, wanting, not wanting—dissatisfaction. We acknowledge both suffering and its originating causes.

We are practicing the fourth noble truth in our contemplations here, freeing attention's entrapment through inquiry and insight. With grace functioning in us and through us, we can dissipate the mirage of "self" in the clear light of wisdom and come to know the third noble truth for ourselves. The third noble truth is a realized awareness of our own essential nature. Our essential nature has never, even for a moment, been absent. It's Eden, home. Ignorance never heads that way.

ALL OF THE LINKS, or conditions, of dependent arising are intertwined. They're so intertwined, mutually influential, that it takes focused attention to recognize a single conditioning factor in and of itself. Ignorance is conditioned by other links just as they condition and deepen ignorance's rutted habit of turning away, of not seeing. Focused, mindful attention is especially demanded as we seek to recognize ignorance—the ground environment of all the others.

To catch ignorance in the act, to see it operating in our own minds, we need to engage in practices that prepare and allow us to see. Meditation—whatever our form of contemplative practice—allows the mind to quiet, to ingather, to pull attention back from its battering within the conditions of the system of suffering. We cannot see ignorance from within ignorance. We need to step beyond the system of self and see with the wisdom grace grants us. In this sense, we create safe and effective space for our exploration and inquiry.

To create that safe and effective space where wisdom can shine its light on the shadows, we need to formally pause and mindfully surrender our attachment to our patterned habits. We don't try to stop those patterned habits; we simply surrender our willingness to let them grab our attention. We want to watch the patterned dynamics. This is only possible with a mind simply witnessing, a mind of bare awareness, a mind without attachment or identification. Although in ignorance our attention is trapped and bound within illusions, these illusions are not who we are.

As you begin to investigate ignorance within your own mind, it is helpful to aspire to keep a commitment to a daily practice. This daily, rhythmic time in presence, in grace recognized, allows the stability of attention that *can* see to begin to mature and ripen. It allows one of the great gifts of our human life to be used.

When we sit deliberately in this way, we take refuge in grace. We align in the sacred with a willingness to surrender all thoughts and objects of attention that would align us in ego. We offer ourselves to grace as grace offers itself to us. We take refuge and rest in refuge.

In refuge, deep and sincere, grace aligns—as wisdom—with our intention to see. Clear seeing increasingly occurs. Clear seeing is synonymous with awakening—a sane relationship with the truth of each moment.

THE VERY NATURE OF IGNORANCE is blurry, cloudy, muddy. It's a mind filled with the particulates of largely mistaken thoughts, just as the eddy is filled with droppings and bits of debris it keeps re-circling within its cycling boundary.

Because the nature of ignorance is a befogged confusion, seeing ignorance is tricky. Ignorance, as we're discovering, is the willingness to ignore, to look away, to resist seeing. Ignorance is the very ground environment beneath the dynamic interplay of all the conditions of dependent arising. Its pervasive presence paradoxically makes it all the harder to see—it keeps the "isolation" of it as an object of inquiry elusive.

There are skillful means, practices that point us toward the truth and lead us to realization. I can offer some suggestions from the ways I've found helpful to observe the conditions of dependent arising in my own mind. There is great benefit to be had when we carve out the time to engage in contemplative inquiries such as these.

We can begin to discern those functions operating. As we do, we're zooming in on *ignorance*. After taking refuge in the presence of grace, after wholeheartedly holding the intention to see, and after sitting deliberately to ingather attention, we can pay mindful attention to the workings of our own mind. For a few minutes or an hour or a day (over the next few years, were we to so choose), we can sit to observe ignorance in action in each of its various functions. As we do this formally, we cultivate the heightened mindfulness that will allow us, informally, to recognize ignorance in action throughout the day.

One way to begin to recognize ignorance operating in our own minds is by looking for its traits, its specific functions. We have, at least conceptually, acquainted ourselves with quite a few of ignorance's various functions. The functions we've discussed include serving as ground environment, fueling the cycle, assuming the truth of assumptions, constricting the attention, obscuring clarity, resisting or turning away, the allowing of illusion, and the blocking of grace.

We want to catch ignorance functioning as the ground environment, allowing the entire cycle of dependent arising to continue over and over. Once the mind has stilled, and we can begin to witness the mind's arisings rather than identifying with them, we can ask with each arising: What is this? Is it muddied? Is it clear? Does it feel stable? How does it shift? Does it feel enlivening or deadening? What about it is captivating to attention? What does it resist?

We can ask, with ignorance as the ground environment: What am I missing? What has ignorance been hiding? Try letting go of mental images. What remains? What lies beyond ignorance?

Try catching ignorance at work. Catch it in operation. Observe how it keeps our sense of self limited and our attention bound within the distortions of its view. See if you can discern this as soon as you sense it has occurred. As our mindfulness is honed and sharpened, we become increasingly able to "freeze frame" moments and can begin to discern the arising of ignorance in the very moment of its occurrence.

Recognize the desire *not* to look too deeply as ignorance. Recognize the arising thoughts that attempt to seduce us back into the cycle.

Recognize the difference between mindfulness and mindlessness.

Simply note, without judgment, the force of ignorance's conditioning. We can note, with ignorance functioning as ground environment, the absence of wonder, the absence of a sense of presence, the absence of illumination. Ignorance has an ennui—a kind of "been there, done that" quality. Newness, freshness, have no chance—nor does genuine delight. As Goethe noted in *Faust*, in the "crystallization" of our habit patterns, "no novelty on earth can make surprise."

Just witness. These dynamics go on in every human mind. It's important, in terms of awakening the only mind we can awaken, to recognize them in our own mind. Recognize that—beyond functioning to obscure it—these dynamics have nothing to do with our essential nature.

Another way to zoom in on ignorance at work is to focus on its function of fueling the cycle of dependent arising. With steadied attention, we can bear witness to ignorance's complicity in keeping the cycle of craving and becoming going. We can note its seductive calls to us, trying to lure attention out of stillness and back into samsara's ongoing churning. Just watch. Just sit for a while and watch. Observe what ignorance wants to allow to continue, what it fuels. No judgment is needed. We're simply intent upon seeing. Sit for a while, if you like, in the awareness in which seeing occurs.

As we've discussed, another of the functions of ignorance is assuming the truth of its own unexamined assumptions. We can sit with quieted mind and ask what mistaken beliefs and unexamined assumptions have flourished like mushrooms in the darkness ignorance casts. Just watch; let those beliefs and assumptions flow. We would never have the time in our lives to list all of our unexamined assumptions.

Just watch. Don't censor. Watch the thoughts rather than thinking the thoughts, as is our usual mode. Our assumptions go from the very most superficial to the most foundational. It's stunning to see what ignorance has allowed to take root, what deeply mistaken and unproven and unprovable notions we've come up with as rules to live by. Simply watch. These are the assumptions of ignorance.

We can ask ourselves, what unmindful thoughts have I allowed to hijack this precious experience of a human life? What are my illusions about my "self" and the possibility of fulfillment?

Remember, as you engage in this inquiry, that it is wisdom (the willingness to see) looking at ignorance (the unwillingness to see). Wisdom can free our agreement and entrancement with any condition. Seeing through any one of the conditions crumbles the entire paradigm that had so entrapped and deceived attention.

Ignorance, we know at least conceptually, constricts our attention. Attention is an expression of boundless awareness, of the sacred. Attention's natural home is in presence, in Being. Within the system of dependent arising and particularly under the influence of ignorance, attention becomes trapped and constricted within the web of influences. To have a more direct experience of ignorance in action, we can sit and note the constriction of attention in our thoughts and in our bodies. We can note the congestion of ignorance as it collapses vastness into a tiny, dense, crowded point of reference.

Constricted attention is like living inside a house with no doors or windows—a closed box. I've compared ignorance to having a smartphone that we perpetually keep on airplane mode, limiting access to all beyond what is already there. To be under the sway of ignorance is to live an infinitely diminished life, a life with limited options.

In this moment, pause. Check to see if you can detect the presence of ignorance in this moment in the constriction of your thoughts and the constriction of your body. This is the experience of being bound. Open to what it feels like to be limited, what it's like to feel alienated, cut off and separate. We can think, what might I learn beyond this constriction? What might be healed? What might be liberated?

The earmarks of ignorance are tension and complexity. Feel the pull of ignorance—as it plucks attention out of simplicity and silence it pulls us into complexity and noisy conceptualizing. We really want to learn to recognize its presence, to see through it. We want to know it as thoroughly as Keith Jarrett came to know each key on his piano.

We can also catch a clear view of ignorance as it functions to obscure and befog. It's helpful, after some silent sitting that quiets the mind, to think of an issue in your life that's been problematic for you lately.

Pause and listen to the words of the thoughts stating the problem. Where does your clarity become blurry? When ignorance is holding sway, thinking itself becomes a swarm of circling, recycling thoughts that will never lead to clarity. The thoughts of ignorance are non-productive in terms of clear seeing. They obfuscate. They're blurry in the way that a fogbank blurs the landscape.

This very blurriness indicates the presence of ignorance in action. This blurriness is a great red flag, a warning that attention is lost in samsaric illusions. The blurriness, the elusiveness, the mental confusion is ignorance's willingness to ignore at work. Ignorance functions as a smokescreen, allowing aspects of the situation to be ignored, to remain unconscious, unseen, elusive.

When we feel caught in the tight and confusing knot of a problem, we can rest assured that the befogging, complicating force of ignorance is at play. Ignorance functions to hide that which it would wish not to see, that which might stop the whole spinning cycle. Simply note it as it arises. This is how attention gets trapped in what we have imputed as "problem." There is no clarity within our mental image of "problem"— just circular thoughts without any hope for wisdom's resolution.

Note what "givens" seem obvious to you in the problematic situation you're contemplating. Question those clarities, those assumptions. Look at what remains unexamined and note the fuzzy state of confusion and complexity that ignorance bestows upon our inquiry, binding attention in the process. Keep looking. Your willingness to see is like a lighthouse in the fog. It's a lifesaver.

Ignorance has a powerful, ingrained, conditioned tendency to resist looking, a habituation to look away. The energetic force of this turning away gives the entire cycle of self and suffering another spin. It spins the wheel. It creates the speedy blur that appears as a continuity, like the individual frames in an animated film.

We can pay mindful attention to where we feel that wish to turn away. We can become mindful of ignorance's resistance to seeing what we do not wish to see. Perhaps it's signs of infidelity or signs of falling in love or signs of aging. Perhaps we do not want to see our dependence or another opinion or the violence and suffering in the world around us. These observations of ignorance's willingness to turn away are at a fairly superficial level—although each urge to look away has deep and tangled roots.

We can look deeper to see ignorance operating in these minds of ours. For example, what do I not want to acknowledge about myself? What am I not ready to admit about my life? To what illusions do I still wish to cling?

What do I not want to know? From what thoughts and emotions do I turn away? From what aspects of my body? From what aspects of truth do I turn away? What am I afraid of? Where am I afraid to look?

Simply note without judgment the power ignorance has amassed to create turning away such a habitual, almost automatic gesture. We ingrain the choice not to see. With mindful attention, we can recognize how the very turning away perpetuates and propels the cycle of self and suffering from which we long to be liberated.

Simply sit. Simply witness for a while. And note the turning away tendency throughout the day. And, when you do note it, watch how—in the moment of seeing—it ceases.

We can watch the moment-by-moment functioning of ignorance as it wreaks its havoc. We can witness the force of its function to allow illusions. Ignorance lets illusions through the security line without a thorough search. Ignorance obscures the processes involved in the formation of an egoic self, our "I"-illusion.

Ignorance needs to be functioning for us to assume a separate sense of self. A good rule of thumb is that if "I" am here, so is ignorance. Play with this in your meditation and throughout the day. See if you can recognize the possibility that this might be so. It can be immeasurably helpful to clearly discern the co-arising of ignorance and the egoic sense of separate self.

Watch the "I"-thought arise again and again. Recognize that every time it does, this is ignorance. This is the most direct way to witness elusive ignorance. It arises with an intense sense of subjectivity. It appears with "my" nametag. It allows the illusion of "self," the illusion of comfort, and the illusion of the future fulfillment of hope.

Sit observing the operations of ignorance in your mind for as long as you like. We can be sure the "I"-thought will be the thought that makes the most frequent appearance. It underlies every other thought and it has layers of "I" ramifications within it—questions of worth, reactions to our wounds, festering blame, and deadening shame, for example. Stay with looking. Discern the ramifications of "I" in your own mind.

In this way, recognizing the "I" as the owner of suffering, we can see that ignorance is foundational in continuing to support and subscribe to the sense of self that suffers, to the sense of self that is separate from others and separate from grace. Ignorance functions to perpetuate the eddy's mistaken sense of identity. It misrepresents the tenuousness and insubstantiality of the self, a "self" that only arises as a byproduct or harmonic of the entire functioning set of conditions. Ignorance holds the "self" as real.

And here's one last suggestion for a way to stare down ignorance by grabbing hold of one of its traits and function: focus on ignorance as the *barrier* between who we think we are and the grace that is already—and always has been—our essential nature.

We can explore what we hold to be our boundaries. Ignorance has placed them there. Where are they? Where do I begin? Where do I end? What are the boundaries of "me"? Where are "others?" Where do "others" exist?

Where is grace? Where is grace relative to where "I" am? What are my beliefs about being "other" than grace—at a distance from it, cut off from it? What is there that separates my innermost experience of life from grace except for ignorance? Stay with the questioning for a while. Let the questions arise from your heart. Look. Note. See through ignorance. And rest in the seeing through.

WITH SUCH PRACTICES of inquiry we can come to wholeheartedly cultivate the intention to become familiar with the functioning— the "frequency," if you will—of ignorance. Its frequency is easily discernible from the frequency of wisdom once we tune into those subtle discriminations.

The presence of ignorance can be discerned when tension and a sense of confusion or complexity arise. Its presence is indicated by beliefs and "convictions." Ignorance is the prerequisite for anything to be believed in—especially to believe in a separate, inherently existing self. Beliefs flourish in ignorance. They dissolve in the light of wisdom. In the light of wisdom, direct realization is all that remains.

We bind ourselves ever more tightly in knots when we allow or rely upon ignorance to try to "figure out" the *mysterium tremendum* of grace. Ignorance functions "above the neck"—in the head, in conceptuality. We hand conceptuality a misplaced and misguided allegiance. May we all become more at ease with resting in stillness at the level of our hearts. Ignorance is absent at the level of the heart. At the heart, in ignorance's absence, stand revealed wonder and wisdom and presence, effortlessly pouring forth their flowing streams of love and compassion.

Just as ignorance—ever unwilling to look—hides and obscures, wisdom illuminates. As it illuminates, the trance is broken. We become dispassionate, disenchanted. We wake from sleepwalking and surrender begins to arise spontaneously. This can never occur within ignorance.

We can hold the intention to surrender our blind commitment to ignorance in all of its future arisings. We don't need to be able to do that fully and completely at the moment. We simply need to cultivate the intention.

Grace is our most cooperative friend.

12

Karmic Formations

KARMIC FORMATIONS is another condition within the cyclic patterning of dependent arising. Along with every other condition, it gives
rise to both "self" and suffering. It sets the stage and tilts the scale,
determining the arisings it gives form to.

Understanding and clearly seeing the power we grant karmic formations (or any of the conditions) when unmindful can be key to shut-
ting down the whole system of mutually dependent conditions. As
we continue our explorations and contemplation, we will increasingly
come to recognize that seeing through even one condition can collapse the entire cycle of suffering, liberating attention from within it.

The condition, karmic formations, is called *saṃskāra* in Sanskrit. One
literal translation is "together maker." This condition functions as "the
churner of forms." Karmic formations—together with ignorance—give
rise to the appearance of a self and to the attitudes, tendencies, urges,
memories, and assumptions held within that subjectivity.

Karmic formations function as memory-based imprints or impres-
sions that shade each present moment's new arising with habitual
patterning. We can think, for example, of the circumstances of weather,
of meteorological conditions, to get a sense of how formations affect
the arising of appearances.

The Rocky Mountains, that long beautiful snowcapped ridge, necessarily elevates the currents of winds traveling past it. The winds must rise over the Rockies to continue their journey eastward on this spinning globe. When the wind currents get to the Rockies' eastern slopes—and with the mountains themselves acting as barriers to their free flow—the winds are too high to clear the air beneath it. As a consequence, a frequent haze caps Denver.

Or, we can think of our water jewels, the beautiful Great Lakes. As winter winds sweep down from the Arctic over the plains of western Canada, the formation of the lakes fills the atmosphere with moisture. Then hitting the formation of landmass, ridiculous amounts of snow are dumped in upstate New York.

This condition of habituated tendencies and grooved patterns gives determining shape and flavor to our experience. Karmic formations impresses our perceptions and conceptions of grace's constant unfolding with its imprints.

Karma is often misunderstood simply in terms of a kind of "payback." A more accurate understanding of karma goes something like this: Our good fortune is based on past wholesome actions; our misfortune is based on past harmful actions. Although it is a notion quite often misrepresented, misunderstood, and sometimes abused, there is indeed truth to this. As we mature on our spiritual paths, we can recognize this in our own experience.

We can think of how our efforts, aided by grace, to cultivate "positive" qualities—such as gratitude, forgiveness, love, compassion, and equanimity, for example—have "softened" us, have "sweetened" us. Our desire to cultivate these noble qualities leaves our boundaries a bit more porous, our defendedness a bit more "at ease," our prejudices vastly diluted. We can see how actions leave an imprint, etching a groove for future actions to follow in a path that has been cleared by past actions. Even on a neurological level, there is evidence of transformation.

Conversely, aided by ignorance and craving, our "negative" thoughts and actions—those that are harmful—arise from past tendencies toward negative thoughts and actions. These harmful thoughts and actions create an easy breeding ground for more of the same. We can think of our anger, our scorn, our rejection, our jealousy, our indifference. Each time we unmindfully act upon those impulses, we raise the odds that we will act in such a way again.

Like rolling a snowball down a hill, we increase the momentum, the force of this condition with each mindless, unwise action of body, speech, and mind. The agenda of karmic formations—movements of mind, movements of meaning and information—is to continue the cycle of the system. This is the agenda of any system.

This is the way karmic formations function. As harmful thoughts and actions are allowed to proceed unchecked, we increase the odds that we will act in such a way again. In addition to that, we further crystallize the separate self-sense in so doing, leaving attention even more deeply bound in self and suffering. We can understand how this is so by recognizing that our reactivities—in the form of either attachment or aversion—seem to validate the "real" existence of a "someone" who is reacting. This confirms and deepens our conviction in the existence of an "I"-illusion existing separately from the assumed object of our reactivity.

Anyone who has engaged in contemplative practice for a while recognizes that awakening stirs our shadows. As our commitment to awaken grows and we continue along a spiritual path, much rises to the surface that can no longer be shut down and hidden in ignorance, in unconsciousness. With our harmful thoughts and actions, we create a future scenario in which we must face the painful regret for the ways in which we've behaved. Our actions, unexamined, actually put more suffering into the system already involved in creating suffering. That's worth pausing to consider.

So, yes, "karma" can be understood in terms of reaping what we sow. Karmic formations, the condition, though, refers even more broadly and subtly to the habituated tendencies, reactivities, proclivities, unexamined assumptions, and memories that, with their varying agendas, create the moment-by-moment movements of our minds, shaping our experience of living.

Karmic formations include such things as the worldviews of the time and culture in which we were raised, the language we use to articulate the world, the assumptions we were spoon-fed by family, church, neighborhood, and school; the experiences we had as a child and the conclusions we came to as a consequence. We were born into an era and a worldview that is secular and "scientific," for example. We live in an era stripped of spirit, trained to view only what is "objective" and measurable. We walk through a spiritually impoverished culture so devoid of a sense of the sacred that we have to deliberately go and search for what already surrounds, permeates, and sustains us.

These are the formations that give shape to our experience beneath the cover of ignorance. Each karmic formation has been conditioned by countless previous cycles of the spinning wheel of all the other conditions. These are the rutted habit patterns of our lives. They have energetic heft.

Karmic formations, in addition to being deeply grooved and imprinted habits, have motivated impulses, vested interests. They have a momentum, pointing ignorance toward form and maintaining movement away from the formless awareness beyond its closed paradigm. They, along with the other conditions, function to create the appearance of a "self"—the someone we believe ourselves to be. Karmic formations keep the eddy, as eddy, going.

Thinking of karmic formations in this way, it becomes easy to recognize these formations as the baggage we carry. These are the habits in which our attention is enslaved. Think of our daily rounds, the routine of them, our predilection for routine. Think of the unexamined assumptions that fill our minds at every moment. Whether we are aware of them or not, they weigh on us and take their hourly toll. "I need to," "I must," "I should," "I'd better" are stones in the suitcase. "I think x," "I want y," "Don't threaten my z" are the burdens we agree to assume. The swirl of our mental imperatives whizzes by so fast, we can barely hear the words that sap our energy and pollute our peace.

Karmic formations work to condition new arisings of "self" from memories of "self"—from bodily, emotional, and mental memories or fabrications of who we believe and have believed ourselves to be. So, included in the functioning force of this condition are our wounds and shadows, our strategies and props.

Pause here, if you like. It is more than worth our time to take an honest look at our remaining wounds.

Spending time to deliberately contemplate and open to our wounds—wounds that can range from tender spots and bruises to deep scar tissue and deeper "holes"—can in itself be healing and transformative. Touching these wounds, take care to bathe them in the wise and tender compassion that is the sweetness of our essential nature.

Take some time as well, if it suits you, to inquire into your shadows. In a sense, that's fairly straightforward work once we've ingathered our attention and opened to exploration. We locate our shadows in our projections. Our shadows are all those aspects of ourselves— both noble and ignoble—for which we have not yet accepted radical accountability. Look at what we project on others. We can see where we project aspects of ourselves, unflattering to our ego, onto others and then react—with anger or aversion or condescension—to what we believe we see. Actually, all we're doing is reacting to our own mental images, our own mental fabrications. Sit, if you so choose, and allow yourself to see this clearly.

We project positive qualities, as yet unowned, onto others as well. When we remain within the orbit of ignorance and the whole system of suffering, we fail to recognize that we could not know goodness in another if we did not also have it in ourselves. We would not recognize the sacred were we not already inseparable from it.

It's helpful for us, too, to examine the strategies of our egoic personality, to inquire into them. Do we smile, control, acquiesce, avoid confronting, harmonize, dominate? Our strategies are our karmic formations in action, both in the world and in our own inner dialogue. Take some time to investigate the ways in which you try to "work" the world.

What strategies do you typically use to try to "work" yourself? Which are genuinely beneficial, bringing you closer to a more sane, awakened relationship with life? Which keep you bound in ignorance and suffering? How well are your strategies actually working? Are they hiding grace or revealing its ever-presence? What do the strategies reveal about who you believe yourself to be?

Again, to get a clear sense of the condition, *karmic formations*, in action, take a look at the "props" in your life. What do you consider necessary? Who do you consider necessary? What self-image do you work to maintain? What happens when the props fail you—or disappear? What remains?

Each question can lead to a new question until we simply end up in silence and the believed need for props and strategies dissolves within the silence.

Karmic formations operate misleadingly, suggesting that here and now can be "tweaked." This condition seductively offers old reactivities to ignorance's hope for a better outcome, one that promises to satisfy craving in the future. Karmic formations, in filtering our present through our past, step away from reality. When this happens, we step away from here and now. Richard Rohr reminds us "there is no elsewhere."

And, yet, we continue to follow the lead of these blind, impersonal, conditioning patterns. Our reactivities are so knee-jerk and blind, so deeply rooted in karmic formations that we, at times, find someone attractive because of a pheromonal response arising from genetically instilled karmic formations. We might meet someone at a gathering and instantly feel aversion because something about the new acquaintance reminded us of someone who mistreated us in third grade— karmic formations from our childhood. Ignorance, and all the other intricately connected conditions of dependent arising, allow some fairly untrustworthy drivers to take the wheel.

It is helpful to our own process of awakening to simply pause and watch our own karmic formations in action. One way to summon them to center stage is to recall—one by one—the people in your life. Do this for a while and you will shortly note that your mental image of each person you're recalling has an attitude based on emotional memories. Who do we actually see fresh? Who do we actually see as they are?

Try this with a mental image of yourself. Picture yourself in your mind's eye. This shouldn't be difficult. We do it mindlessly, haphazardly, a thousand times a day. Do it now deliberately, if you like, and dozens of facets of the karmic formations amassed around your "I"-illusion will pop into place. See them. One by one. See through them. And rest in the spaciousness beyond karmic formations' heavy hand. We do not need to remain lost and bound in a form-only experience of life, bound by self-reference.

Unbound, we move into the endless possibility of grace. Isn't that our heart's yearning?

When will we finally acknowledge that we are "worthy" of that for which we've loved all along—and that which has loved us all along?

WE HAVE, as we practice, a growing recognition that karmic formations is the keeper of assumptions. It is an incredibly beneficial exercise to take the time to actually write down our unexamined assumptions, our endless beliefs, opinions, and imperatives. My own assumptions include conviction about the correct way to decorate a Christmas tree. They include a progressive bias, understanding full well that the general adoption of my view would create a better world. I also most often believe that the "I" who owns my house exists inside a body I also own.

Try this exercise of inquiry, if you like. Literally—just list the assumptions you hold. Cloaked by ignorance, these assumptions seem so clear and true. They arise in such declarative sentences—so sure of themselves.

We can often instantly see their absurdity when the words baldly appear in black and white. When we write them out or share them aloud with a friend, we see them without the clouding distortions of ignorance. As we list them, we can acknowledge that these are the karmic formations that have been running the show, shaping the situations of our lives.

And look at your list with focused, mindful attention. Take your capacity to believe back from investment in them. To the degree that you can, do this lightly. Let yourself laugh or at least smile with the freeing of attention that had been bound in belief. Reclaim the power you've given them. They have disenfranchised us from our own essential nature, from our true home.

When we do this, we start to let go of some of the baggage and start to travel a bit lighter. Letting go—surrender—is key to freeing attention from bondage in self and suffering. We let go by meeting habitual patterns with a still mind of equanimity. We surrender attachment to them when we simply witness them without reactivity, assent, or identification.

Recognizing these karmic formations as "running the show," we can come to see that they are volitional; they have an agenda. They are in service to craving and craving's wish to have the entire samsaric cycle continue. Fueled by craving and the false promises of ignorance, the cycle is always chasing that elusive gold ring, the happiness that always eludes the separate sense of self.

The condition, *karmic formations*, functions in service to the condition, *craving*. The formations hold the seeds of "self" and the seeds for craving's specific appetites or agendas. Within the cycle of self and suffering, karmic formations conditions four attachments. We are conditioned to be attached to sensual desires, to views (our opinions and ways of seeing things), to rites and rituals (the ways we think things should be done), and to our sense of self. Pausing to contemplate each of these seeds is beneficial. Unexamined, they leave us with endless opportunities to keep attention bound ever more deeply in samsara.

After taking the time to center in quiet mind, we can ask: How attached am I to sensual pleasures of food and drink and pleasing objects and the illusory joys of frivolousness? How much of my life has been spent in search of what I believe to be pleasure or comfort or beauty? If I were to construct a pie chart of time spent following my attachments to sensual desires and comfort, would I want anyone else to see it? Finally, we can ask, Where has my attachment to sensual desire led me—into grace or into suffering?

The revered Buddhist monk Thich Nhat Hanh says that "attachment to views is the greatest impediment to the spiritual path." We can explore how attached we are to our entrenched views and opinions. We can inquire, if we choose: What is my experience when my views and opinions are challenged? Or confronted? Or dismissed? Or ridiculed? How deep is my conviction that my view is a "better way"? What fears do I have that my present views and opinions might not be true, after all? How resistant am I to exploring that? Where would the absence of assumptions leave me? What would that mean?

We can ask: How attached am I to rites and rituals? What superstitious beliefs do I impute upon rites and rituals? Is there a problem if I meditate without offerings for example or stretch my leg in a formal sitting or if I take part in a Catholic mass officiated by a woman priest? It is in our attachment to rites and rituals that so many get caught in a lesser and limited understanding of all a wisdom tradition has to offer in terms of authentic transformation.

Our attachment to rites and rituals comes into play in more secular ways, as well. Karmic formations govern "the correct way to load a dishwasher," for example. They also govern our thinking about food, parenting, and a perceived "requirement" to stand for the national anthem. We can think: Which of my habits and routines—the rites and rituals of my daily life—do I not want disturbed?

Karmic formations impress thoughts, emotions, and the habits of the body in accordance with memories, forming a someone from those memories. These mental formations are the structural beliefs of the paradigm of self—fabricated patterns that ignorance allows to remain unexamined. These beliefs maintain the multiple self-referential loops that continue the cycle, keeping us ever an eddy—isolated and tenuous in our mistaken separation.

We can look at our conditioned proclivity to subjectivity, to existing as *someone*, to our own "I"-illusion. Can I even risk imagining that "I" exist as illusion? Try, if you like. See what arises. Who am I if I'm not who I believe I am? Try imagining life without endless self-reference.

And rest in the unbounded imagining.

OUR GENETIC LEGACY is an aspect of karmic formations. Our human body and our human mind, our placement in families and class within culture, our tendencies to resilience or anxiety, our intellectual capacity, our opposable thumb, our physical strength, our language, our eyesight, our appearance—these are all karmic formations. Ten thousand years ago, a heavy-breasted, wide-hipped woman was considered the ultimate in beauty. The karmic formation of that body type has a different significance and experience in an anorexic era—that anorexic era, itself, a conditioned phenomenon. Think of your racial heritage. Has that karmic formation granted you immense, valuable, covert privilege, or a disadvantage that can prove fatal?

Our genetic legacy includes the karmic formations of human minds over millennia. Karmic formations condition the tendency for us to exist as pleasure-seeking beings. Has this not been the story of our lives for the most part—pleasure seeking? For many of us, this pre-dilection is carried along on our spiritual path. How many "highs" have we yearned to recreate? How does our egoic self-sense picture its "enlightenment"? This force of pleasure seeking strengthens and con-ditions our craving and the desperation we often feel around craving.

The condition of karmic formations holds the "seed" of self that is brought into appearance by the web of all conditions. It includes the predisposition toward an egoic self-sense, an agenda for becoming *someone*. Karmic formations functions as a powerful factor in the devel-opment of an ego identity. We're used to that separate sense of self.

The condition, *karmic formations*, includes every survival imper-ative. Every survival imperative is binary—resting on the implicit assumptions of "I" and "other," threat or benefit. In a world free of predators the survival imperative, designed to protect the physical organism, now functions in service to the self-sense.

Karmic formations have been conditioned by every previous crav-ing for an egoic identity, every movement toward becoming a separate sense of self, every momentary birth of a separate sense of self, and every aging and death of that temporarily appearing "I"-illusion.

How many births and deaths have we each placed the nametag "I" upon? How many iterations of "me"? Me 3.0? Me 24.0? Me 79.0? Inquiry into this very question can result in one of the transforming "aha" moments of a lifetime.

One of my own most illuminating—and humbling—examples of placing the nametag occurred on a plane. My granddaughter had downloaded the card game hearts on my iPhone so I could play on the long flight. I opened the app, found the playing field of four players—"left bot," "top bot," "right bot," and the bottom one, which was labeled "you." Instantly, truly, it dawned that "you" meant "ME!" and the "I"-illusion entered in full force.

I utterly identified with a virtual position on a programmed game on a small technological device while flying 35,000 feet above the earth in a plane. It was exhilarating, a rush—it was "ME!"

It got worse. One of the cards you generally want to avoid receiving in the game of hearts is the queen of spades. When the "left bot" passed that card to the place marked "you"—which I knew was "ME!"—I was miffed. I could feel the slight spite in the urge to pass that card right back in "left bot's" direction on the next round. "I" and my reaction arose in relationship to a sequence of computer code.

No wonder we have riots and divorces and stymied governments and wars. These tendencies run deep and will jump in, in the blink of an eye, in the most innocent seeming situation.

One of the ways to see karmic formations in action is to simply sit and note the arising of the "I"-thought, our most repeated and ingrained karmic formation. Sit quietly for about twenty minutes, if you like, and do a simple body scan. You'll note sensations in your body. They always rise and fall, appear, and dissolve. They morph. Just like everything else, they're energy in flux and transformation.

Note the tendency—arising from ignorance and karmic formations along with all the other conditions—to instantly note "my" neck or "my" back or "my" aching knee. We instantly place not only egoic identity—"I"—but a sense of ownership—"mine"—upon an arising sensation. Note the mental template we hold about "my" body—its position in space, its silhouette, its spatial referents, its imagined boundaries within our fabricated blueprint.

We can recognize that mental template, a karmic formation, deepening the conviction that the body exists in the way we conceive it. We also have some nebulous, unexamined notions that we own it, and even more unexamined notions that mind exists inside the body. When we begin to recognize the mental template of our body in the stillness of our meditation, we realize that the body exists inside the mind.

As you sit, noting what arises, recognize the thought "I" or "mine" every time it appears. This is not to go to war with the thought but simply to understand how it arises, to see through the spinning dynamics of dependent arising. Catch the "I"- illusion as karmic formations condition it to appear.

Catch the "I"-illusion as it conceives of itself to be catching the "I"-illusion. And rest. Just let go. It has always been an illusion. We've been fooling ourselves for a long time. There is no "I" to let go of. We simply want to see through the mistaken belief in it. That belief utterly interferes with the recognition of our own goodness and vastness.

I've had to chuckle many a time in meditation as my sense of self conceives itself to be surrendering to and taking refuge in grace, turning the entire contemplative experience over to grace. I do this with all the sincerity my ego can muster. Then the insight dawns that there is no "I" to surrender anyway. What's "released" is an illusion and what's recognized is that grace has been manifesting all along as that morning's practice—including the appearance of surrendering and taking refuge. The system of dependent arising churns out the "I"-illusion again and again, but it has no power when met with the lightness and equanimity of a mind with no wish to cling.

As ONE OF THE CONDITIONS in the patterned interplay of dependent arising's cycle, karmic formations function to overlay the past upon the present. Under the cover of ignorance, imprints from the past confiscate the present. Without mindfulness, we allow this squandering of the finite moments of our precious human life.

Karmic formations take the arising of each present moment and impress their old and fixed proclivities upon freshness. They shape arisings, just as an embossing instrument impresses its shape upon paper or as the manmade canyons of a great city funnel and amplify the wind.

In this way, the condition of karmic formations can be seen as a determining force, giving shape through its very presence as a condition to each and every arising within the closed system. It gives a distinctive quality to our experience—and, as we've seen, karmic formations has agendas.

We can think of the predominant, the most frequent, thoughts and states of mind that have arisen lately. Is it a tendency to anger or pride? Is there a flavor of worry or selfish ambition? Do we have hopes and concerns about loved ones whose lives would be so much better if they only listened to us? Are there frequent questions of self-worth? How predominant is fear?

These are our habit patterns, our karmic formations. You can check to see what impulses have been running your life lately. They are old and familiar, based upon many an unexamined assumption.

It can be freeing to simply note the dynamic of karmic formations in your mind, to note attention's willingness to unquestioningly follow its lead. Insight arises when we see where our attention has a predisposition to lean, to acquiesce. We see the impersonal habits that have been so deeply imprinted. We can begin to discern the agenda of the predisposition, the volitional aspect of karmic formations. When we can note what the egoic sense of self believes it can gain in this moment's situation, we can see the very workings of dependent arising.

Karmic formations are powerful determining forces. Buddha called them "the tide of conceivings." Christian contemplative Martin Laird speaks of "the ordeal of thoughts." We can note them all day long in our most frequent thoughts, our most familiar desires and emotions, our most habitual actions. Stay mindful. That mindfulness will prevent them from usurping attention and keeping it trapped in the wheel of self and suffering.

Our own karmic habits often manifest as guilt we carry, or the animosity we feel toward someone we believe has harmed us. We can begin to erode some of the energetic, conditioning power of these karmic formations with a simple, heartfelt forgiveness practice.

A forgiveness practice for ourselves allows us to learn what is to be learned from the past action and its consequences. This learning is objective, not condemnatory. It can be redemptive if undertaken with sincerity. This is a noble practice and we want to engage in it deliberately—with a perfect balance of dignity and humility, with a perfect balance of gratitude and confidence. It's helpful to take the time to center into the meditative equipoise of this balance.

We want to rest in our heart, the love-filled and wisdom-filled abode of grace in this human body. We can take the guilt, self-loathing, and scalding judgments we may hold about ourselves in our mind, and allow this bitterness to simply drop into the compassionate heart. As we engage in forgiving ourselves for actions we regret, we slowly and deliberately—wholeheartedly—allow each regret, with its coating of guilt, to melt in sweet compassion.

A forgiveness practice for others, toward whom we may have animosity, also occurs at the level of the heart. It begins with opening to the anger, resentment, or even hate that has developed. These jagged and hardened reactions can't be sidestepped or ignored or suppressed or denied. Attending to them, we acknowledge them as wounds. We open to them with tender mercy.

After we have been honest—and compassionate—with ourselves about the feelings we've been harboring, we then can turn to our own good heart. We can consider that this person—upon whom we've imputed a word such as *enemy* or *adversary*, or that we have otherwise maligned—is as trapped and lost as we are in their own unique yet universally patterned cycle of self and suffering. That insight softens our hardened animosity. We can recognize—because it's true—that as much as we wish to awaken and free our attention from the bindings of samsara, so too do they. Living beings suffer and, unmindful, we spread our suffering around us.

We can recognize that our animosity arose from our mistaken acquiescence to the "I"-illusion. We took their actions personally. At the most piercing moment of his life, Jesus taught us this: "Father, forgive them for they know not what they do." We can wish them well and from that well-wishing, a stance of equanimity can discern the most healthy way to relate to them—or not—in the future.

In practices such as these forgiveness practices, we erode our karmic formations, just as wind and rain and centuries erode the formation of a mountain. Contemporary mystic Eckhart Tolle notes that "the most important step out of karmic misery is forgiveness." We unburden. We unpack the weighted baggage.

Clearly seeing the arising of karmic formations can break the trance they induce. We can recognize—and it is immeasurably beneficial to do so throughout each day—that with each in-breath, everything that is necessary is given. With each out-breath, everything that is no longer necessary is released. We need only the essential. In continuing to let go and surrender in each moment, we diminish the energetic power of karmic formations to amass, to overlay past upon present, and to continue to forge a future path in the same old direction—back into self and suffering.

As we open and inquire ever more deeply, we come to see that where we've been feeds the shape and flavor of this moment. We come to see that as we more mindfully come to peace with this moment, simply allowing it, we shape where we're going. We can turn the future over to grace in this very moment.

Seeing the "I" maker at work, we can break the cycle. There is a liberation and an emptying of a once-congested mind, now freed for increased communion in grace. This leads to a further dissipation of the walls of alienation, isolation, and separation we have experienced for so long within the cycle of suffering.

As our freed attention moves into formless awareness, grace reveals that neither form nor self are what we held them to be.

We grow in our capacity to open to and recognize liberating truth.

13

Consciousness

As we continue to grow in our understanding of and ability to see through—to penetrate—the conditions that set the stage for the emergence of the "I"-illusion, we increasingly awaken into wise view, the view of things as they are. Our growing mindfulness and clarity, our deepening understanding as we pause to contemplate and inquire, free attention previously trapped within the cycle of ignorance and suffering. This is unbinding. Unbinding involves this liberation of attention; it is another word for awakening.

We're looking at the cycle of suffering to explain and clearly understand it. Without wisdom, when our ordinary minds are confronted with the truth of suffering, we resort to unproductive and unbeneficial stances of despair, resignation, or even a reckless nihilism. Understanding dependent arising, as it functions within our own experience, illuminates a path of liberation. With the obscurations cleared, with the self-emptying of surrender, grace emerges ever more freely and fills the space of our being.

Let's continue looking together at the process that I have and you have—for so long—believed to be who we are. This is the same process that is occurring in this very moment, churning out a sense of self that we each—in all our differences—refer to with the same word: "me."

The third link in the cycle of dependent arising is *consciousness*. It is deeply influenced by ignorance, karmic formations, and all the other conditions of dependent arising. In turn, it deeply influences ignorance, karmic formations, and all the other factors in the confusing, spinning distortions that trap and bind attention.

The meaning of consciousness, in this context, is more than what we typically refer to with the word *sentiency*. Consciousness has a specific meaning here. It refers to a cohering function of attention that is contaminated by ignorance and in service to grasping. It has a strong conditioning role in the causal process giving rise to the "I"-illusion.

Consciousness is the condition that functions to weave an inner sense of consistency and continuity. Its function is enactive—organizational, sense-making, cohering. It provides the feeling of familiarity, the feeling of living in a known world. In many ways, it simplifies life for us and is useful for survival, but it operates without any wisdom. It operates within blind conditioning. Consciousness skates on the surface of appearances, acting on the natural inclination of aversion to chaos.

Consciousness cognizes. It registers perceptions, both mental and physical, links them with memories of previous mental and physical perceptions, and stores the imprints for future reference. These imprints or memories serve as the vehicle creating an illusion of continuity. Needless to say, the memory of "I" predominates. Consciousness is not analytical in the sense of having any inclination or capacity to inquire "what is this?" Its analytical functioning is conditioned to operate in terms of practicality, of ensuring survival or relevance to the separate sense of self.

Consciousness coordinates the faculties of life-in-form. It coordinates the "consciousness" of the senses—eye consciousness, ear consciousness, nose consciousness, tongue consciousness, tactile consciousness, and mental consciousness—so that our experience of an appearance is one of a unified entity. It apprehends forms as unified entities—including the form of the mental image arising as "me"—and coordinates them within a dualistic worldview determined by the patternings of dependent arising.

Consciousness has a great role in designating self as separate—from others and from the sacred. If we observe carefully, we can come to see that the condition of consciousness also keeps our attention separate from aspects of ourselves—in particular, our shadow aspect. If, for example, a momentary flash of insight reveals a view of self that is "ego dystonic"—in conflict with our preferred or most familiar self-image—it is quickly submerged in the ongoing, effortful rush of consciousness for consistency.

Consciousness involves itself in the screening process that determines what is stored in conceptuality. It works with the assumptions karmic formations holds and ignorance allows. With selective memory, it creates entities out of parts—out of bits of sensory data, binding them in some sense of cohesion.

Consciousness creates the gestalts we experience, the sense that something appears as a whole although it is made of parts. We create gestalts even when parts are missing, as in when we can read a word on a flashing neon sign with letters missing and never blink an eye.

Consciousness is the condition that factors to fill in the blanks and weave over the gaps, without acknowledging that it is doing so. Here, again, we see the influence of ignorance as well as the influence of our karmic formations. In the neon sign with the missing letters, it is our karmic formation of recognizing a known word that leaps to fill in the blanks of the missing letters. It is consciousness that functions to leap.

The speed of this reflexive looping and leaping creates the apparent continuity of the "I"-illusion. The condition, *consciousness*, drives with a heavy foot on the accelerator.

Consciousness, which gives the lived sense of a peaceful security, has the quality of rushing to create that illusion of security. It does this by using formulaic narratives, like a television series that has run for a few too many seasons.

We can catch consciousness at work in just a few minutes of sitting quietly and contemplatively, observing the movements of our own minds. Try this for a bit, if you like. The point of this inquiry is to note not only how the appearances to mind wander but how consciousness eliminates any sense of gap between one wandering thought and the next. We don't even notice the gaps. This is the force of the condition, *consciousness*, functioning. It works to effect a seamless weave, an illusion of continuity.

Sit for a while and observe this in action.

THE CONDITION OF CONCIOUSNESS functions as an obscuring force—like ignorance. It skips over all that might be seen were it not so intent upon its mission of weaving a sense of constancy and continuity, a sense of familiarity. It shrouds and conceals the truth of each new moment.

Consider this experiment for a moment. Hold up your hand and look at it. And notice that all that your eyes can see is shape and color, refractions of light. That is the extent of the capacity of the visual organs. Look for a while and check if that is so.

You cannot *see* "hand." You cannot *see* "my hand." "Hand" and "my hand" exist only as gestalts, mental constructs and mental images.

What you are calling your hand—and what you believe you are *seeing*—is in fact your *mental image* of your hand. All that can be seen is shape and color—although even shape and color are largely mentally imputed.

In truth, all we can see are refractions of light, energy in flux and transformation. In the apparent solidity and constancy of the "hand," cells are coming into existence and cells are dying even as you look, microbes are flying in and out, and atoms are spinning.

Consciousness, along with ignorance and karmic formations, is the condition that jumps to the conclusion, "my hand." Stay looking for a few minutes, if you will. Watch the conditioning factor, consciousness, at work.

So many people engaging in this inquiry simply go, "Oh, sure. I get it. All my eyes can see are refractions of light"—and then they quickly jump up and move on to the next moment of unmindfulness. So many treat the "I get it" moment, even if they do actually "get it" for that moment, as if it were merely a quirky fact, as if it were utterly inconsequential. This is what the condition, *consciousness*, does. This is its conditioning function. It leaps over any truth that might bring a halt to the entire spinning system.

In the "my hand" example, many never let the full impact of the implications of what they have just realized touch them. That "my hand" cannot be seen, that we conflate "seeing" with the quick arising of a mental image, has immense paradigm-shattering implications. I often forget them and pay the price in egoic unease.

Consciousness provides the content to awareness and, with the other conditions, traps attention within its patterned cycling, leaving it ensnared in ignorance. Awareness—itself sacred and always available in the spacious gaps consciousness rushes to fill—is never entered, never known.

Think of the thousands of opportunities grace has offered each of us in our lives, offerings that we've let sink like stones in the ocean. Think of the insights and revelations we've had in our lives that we've let slip away beneath the obscuring force of consciousness. The condition, *consciousness*, blocks the possibility of stabilizing and then embodying the glimpses of truth grace has granted each of us. We can end the blockade with the wisdom of clear seeing.

CONSCIOUSNESS IS THE CONDITION in which all of our self-referential stories arise—where they appear to enduringly (for a time) reside. Consciousness, in its quick and deft weaving of moments and appearances, seems to hold our stories of self within it as fact, as reality. It provides the climate from which subjective experience can arise.

We can pause here for a few minutes, if you like, and see what self-referential narratives we hold to be true, to be accurate accounts of who we are and how things are. We want to look at the "stories" of our lives, the stories ego tells. These are our stories of explanation, justification, shame, blame, pride, and disappointment. Our narratives come in every flavor. Just note the different ones that have become refrains in the decades of your life.

Take some time to do this deliberately, intently.

Note the flavor and the feeling tone of each narrative, noting particularly each of the highlighted moments that appear to justify the narrative. These are the qualities we believe define us. We can ask what thoughts are firing in this moment? What thoughts fuel the rutted narrative? How is this narrative sustaining the "I"-thought? How is it assenting to ignorance?

Having noted the narratives, note how they ignore whatever insights and revelations we've been blessed to receive. Note how they turn us away from the light and back into the shadow of self. Note what power we've given them. And rest in the awareness that—beyond the stories— is noting the stories. Rest in awareness for a while, refreshing your being.

MINDFUL OF THE ENERGETIC FORCE of consciousness, we can notice it in action throughout the day, and not just in formal meditative or contemplative practice. It rushes to conclusions. It blocks scrutiny and analysis. It provides the distorted information that ignorance accepts.

Think of our stereotypes and our generalizations, for example. They're hothouses where our attachments and aversions—aspects of the condition of craving—flourish. It is helpful to see this—up close and personal—in our own minds. We can ask ourselves, what stereotypes and generalizations have I been willing to cosign? How powerfully do they work to sustain the sense of separation from others? Do they have any relationship whatsoever to the truth of interbeing, the truth of our interconnection on every level? Do they turn me back toward ignorance, or toward wisdom?

Consciousness conspires with ignorance to hide the light of the momentary gaps between newly arisen moments. This is the light where wisdom resides, the light that can serve as the platform for attention's release from limitation. Having spent some deliberate contemplative time coming to recognize consciousness at work, we can also begin to watch it at work throughout the day. It often has us three miles down the road from here and now in a story about someone we don't like, or a scenario we hope might come to be. Consciousness daydreams. It is not awake.

We live our lives in mental reference, in fabricated illusion. It is humbling to recognize that dogs do the same thing when they bark furiously at—or back away in fear from—their own reflection in a mirror. It's only a difference of degree.

Consciousness misconstrues; it even misconstrues "now," fabricating a mistaken meaning, a mistaken understanding that keeps us from presence. I once asked someone I was working with in a deep growth-work setting how she was doing "right now." She talked about how she had been doing for the past few weeks and how she anticipated she'd be doing in the next few weeks. I kept inviting and encouraging her to narrow down what she called "now," to come to the sliver of its fresh and cutting edge.

Her mind, with ignorance operating, could not compute such a freeze-framed present. Her mind, with the condition of consciousness operating, resisted the gap of light and wisdom each moment of presence offers. I say this with compassion and without judgment. The only way I could have observed what I observed was from knowing those dynamics in my own mind, recognizing how I have so often lost my bearings in mistaken mental reference.

May we come, with commitment and the blessings of grace, to penetrate consciousness' daydreams and fabrications. May we all come to recognize, as did Nisargadatta, that we have "enclosed ourselves in time and space," squeezed ourselves "into the span of a lifetime and the volume of a body," thus creating "the innumerable conflicts of life and death, pleasure and pain, hope and fear."

For our own sake, for each other, for the sake of the world, may we all quickly awaken. Just as we arise from sleep each morning, we wake up by opening our eyes.

14

Name-and-Form

WE CAN'T HELP BUT NOTICE that there is still no "I" among the conditions we've explored. There are, though, plenty of causes and conditions lining up and coalescing to give rise to its appearance. Let's look at the fourth link involved in setting the stage for the debut.

Name-and-form is the next condition Buddha highlighted as he shared his insights into dependent arising. In Sanskrit, the word used for this condition is *nāmarūpa*—*nāma* meaning "name" and *rūpa* meaning "form." I wish there were a more clear and elegant English equivalent. We could call it "labeling," but this condition functions to do more than that. It "holds" the aggregates that we refer to as body and mind—the physical and mental components of human existence that are the bases of all our imputations—and brings them into play. These include feeling, perception, intention, attention, and the physicality—the elements and intricacies—of the human body. "Name-and-form" will have to do.

It is a powerful conditioning force establishing—to our ordinary, conventional minds—both subject and object. It creates the great chasm, the great abyss, of duality that conceptuality believes and perceptions, filtered through conceptuality, agree to support.

Name-and-form, in cooperation with all the other conditions of dependent arising, leads to the mistaken, suffering-prone view of dualism, of separation. It obscures the truth of our nondual interbeing—the very essence of grace—with the misleading yet seductive illusion of a separate, inherently existent "self." Thich Nhat Hanh reminds us that "the idea that there must be a subject hides the truth."

Ignorance creates the seeming abyss of separation; wisdom makes the abyss instantly "dis-appear." May we all grow in that wisdom.

Name-and-form conditions the limitation and entrapment of our attention in a form-only world. Its functioning seemingly severs form from the sacred formless. Ultimately, this is impossible. Form and formlessness—individual manifestation and grace—are inseparable. Within a paradigm of mistaken beliefs, though, this truth is hidden from our attention.

Name-and-form functions to discern, differentiate, emphasize, and bring formation to "the many," rather than to the unified field, the ground of being. It leads attention to get lost in "the many," obscuring the unity manifesting as the entire display. The tendencies of name-and-form keep us from recognizing grace in all of its disguises.

Separation and duality begin with naming. When we remain unmindful and under the spell of ignorance, name-and-form seems to reify the illusory nature of the appearance, seems to establish it as separate and inherently existent.

It's not that we need to aspire to dispense with naming as we go through our daily lives. What will benefit us is naming "lightly"—with spaciousness and with the recognition of name as "mere imputation." We want to hold name-and-form gently—without the tight grip of grasping, without the clutching investment of ownership or hope or hate, without the unexamined belief that label is more than mere label.

Name-and-form brings form into apparent being through labeling, through name. This condition of life-in-form, of the human experience, has enhanced our individual and our species-wide chance of survival. It allows us to distinguish between grace's disguises, enabling us to recognize danger, for example, or opportunity. As a condition operating within ignorance, though, it continually misleads us, separating one thing from another and deepening our unquestioning conviction in isolated entities and duality.

We live in a world where shoes need to be tied, stop signs obeyed, and where umbrellas really are helpful for staying dry in the rain. Our capacity to label appearances to mind serves us in that "conventional" reality, the world of appearances. It is not name-and-form itself, but name-and-form *believed in* that keeps us trapped in the cycle of samsara.

We have, in the course of exploring together, come to recognize that ignorance is a confused relationship with what's so. We have begun together to understand that ignorance lurks behind whatever we take for granted. To believe that appearances conditioned by name-and-form exist in the way they appear is to acquiesce without investigation. To acquiesce without investigation is to remain unmindful, without wisdom—bound.

We need an awakened relationship with the appearances name-and-form bring into being. The entire system of dependent arising produces illusory appearances. It churns them out. Having begun to deliberately engage in the practice of wise view, we now have options other than blind assent to the misapprehension of appearances.

We can begin to recognize that naming form is a helpful convenience and nothing more. We sleepwalk in a dream world of our own creation when we offer blind assent to more than the label.

There's a teaching story that has always moved me. I can't vouch for its historicity, but know it can help to loosen and unravel our blind belief that all phenomena—including the self—exist in the manner in which they appear. It functions in a profoundly revelatory way for me vis-à-vis the illusory, dream-like nature of appearances. I hope it functions in that way for you as well.

Here's the story.

Buddha and one of his disciples are traveling together, from one teaching place to another. At one point in their journey, having traveled many miles, the path they follow wanders close to a nearby brook. Buddha, now in an aging body, asks his young disciple if he would please bring him some water to drink. The young man gladly walks toward the brook and bends down on its shallow bank to cup his hands and let them fill with water to bring back to Buddha.

As he bends, he notices a foot in the brook and lifts his eyes to the beautiful young woman whose foot it is. "Beautiful," he thinks and smiles at her and instantly falls in love. And she, too, falls in love with him. They marry quickly, as is her tribe's custom. "My wife," he thinks and they set up housekeeping in her village on the other side of the brook.

"Our home," they say, is the setting where, in the quick river of time, a son and daughter—both healthy and dearly loved—are born to them. The years pass, the children grow, the couple ages. One day a marauding tribe rushes in and burns the village down. Although he tried to save them, his wife and children perished in the flames. Anguished, he runs to the brook, trying to escape the suffocating smoke.

At its edge, he looks up and Buddha says, "May I have the water now?"

A dream within a dream. Such is the entire system of samsara.

And, yet, even though a dream within a dream, as we awaken

140

we understand that our actions of body, speech, and mind matter greatly. We each have a radical responsibility in the dream we create. The dream we create can add suffering to the world or it can add kindness.

LET'S ZOOM IN together and begin to take a close look at this powerful force of name-and-form as it conspires to set the stage for the emergence of the "I"-illusion, this dream within a dream.

Name-and-form is a creating force within the other conditions of dependent arising. It gives form to appearances. Its operation is conditioned by ignorance, by karmic formations, by consciousness, and by the other conditions of the cycle of suffering.

Along with form come the laws of form. In an important way, the laws of form are the laws of suffering. Form has friction. To the degree that our identification rests only in form, the form we imagine ourselves to be is prone to being grated and shredded—prone to being rubbed against reality until we burst into flame. Again: We call this dukkha, suffering.

I remember once, years ago, in graduate school, being struck by a particular point the professor was making. He was speaking about subtle but fundamental forces within language itself. He asked us to consider the difference between the sentence, "This is a blue sky," and the sentence, "The universe is sky-ing bluely." For me, it was a revelation, a deep moment of insight.

Think of the difference in mindset and worldview and implication and assumption between your own versions: "I am Kathleen" and "right here, the universe is Kathleen-ing." Name-and-form, as a condition affecting the entire system of suffering, has a predilection for the former way of making the statement. The former way is tighter, more closed, more congested, more limiting, more vulnerable to the laws of friction and suffering.

Try it with your own name and experience the difference. Play with it for a bit, if you like, noting the experiential difference in the two articulations.

The two different articulations create two utterly different experiences and understandings of what's happening, of what's possible, and of our own true nature.

Take a moment, if you wish, to explore for yourself which articulation has greater spaciousness for you, greater freedom, a greater sense of grace present. And, to whatever degree you experience a bit more spaciousness and freedom and grace, rest in that ease for a few minutes more.

Let's look at the very act of naming—the function of name-and-form. Let's begin to explore the consequences of casual, unmindful naming. We've examined the beneficial consequences in terms of survival. Let's look at what else is affected and determined by name-and-form.

When we attach to label, we close down the totality of what's happening. We close down the totality of what's possible. I remember watching my own little tribe of young toddlers playing in my office one rainy afternoon. They were playing with a reed basket. They could put it over their heads and stumble into each other, laughing. They could put a foot in it and try to shuffle along across the room. They could sit on it, and they could roll it back and forth to each other. The creative possibilities seemed endless. The custodian walked in and asked what the kids were doing with the garbage can. That was the end of the fun.

When we attach to label, when we believe that the label has some ultimate truth, ignorance collapses vast potentiality to a tiny point of self-referential object. This is how the ever-presence of grace, formless awareness, is lost to both view and experience in a form-only world.

When we name, perceptions follow words. Perceptions acquiesce to words. With our almost constant inner dialogues, we talk our way into separation and into the confusion of believing that the object we name exists as it appears. We talk ourselves into the confusion of believing that the object inherently exists outside of our mind. We talk ourselves into separation.

Form arises as a confirmation of thought, and each of our thoughts is already conditioned by karmic formations. When we name, we only know a mental image. Attention is removed a step or two, or a thousand, from Presence. With name, attention is caught. Resting in mental images, we only know what the mind said the appearance was. We saw this for ourselves when we looked at "my hand."

We miss life loving itself, having compassion for itself, within appearances—as it does naturally and spontaneously when labels are held lightly. When labels are held lightly, grace shines through. Ok-koo Kang Grosjean, a Korean mystic poet, described such a light holding of labeling in this way:

> Taking a walk
> I saw
> a wildflower.
> Not knowing its name
> I saw
> its beauty only.

Imagine how we might live Jesus's injunction to "love one another," how we might embody the Dalai Lama's suggestion to make our practice of religion simply a practice of kindness, were we to hold the labels of "self" and "other" more lightly.

We might then, in every moment, see "beauty only."

TAKE A FEW MOMENTS NOW, if you would. Breathe a few deep, conscious breaths as a way to declare intention in this pause to explore. Because the duration of only a few deep breaths is typically not enough for our minds to deeply quiet, we will be giving ourselves an opportunity to examine our own endless inner dialogue—it has not yet ceased—with the increased mindfulness bestowed by both the breaths and our intention.

Simply sit back and listen to your interior dialogue's flow of thoughts and words, assumptions, and concerns. Catch, if you can, the long, deep tentacles of each word and assumption. Catch all that each word and assumption refers to and includes. "A tangled skein, a thicket," Buddha called it when he observed it in his own mind.

Notice the inner dialogue chatting away. Inner dialogue is our noisy constant commentary. The very presence of our inner dialogue seems to confirm an "I" who is giving the commentary. In fact—check it out if you want—many of us, when unmindful, cling to the inner dialogue as "self."

Think of the convention in cartoons of putting words and thoughts and even symbols of emotions in little bubbles, each with a little "tail" close to a person's head. Our identification with "self" is like identifying with the content of the bubbles. We tend to think of the nonstop chatter and reaction within the bubble as "me."

Who we are is not our inner dialogue. Our inner dialogue is nothing more than words attached to habitual, conditioned neural firings.

Play with this. As much as ego may be tormented by a harsh or anxious inner dialogue, ego fears an existence in which there is no inner dialogue. Who am I without inner dialogue—who am I if the bubble is empty of content? Inner dialogue supports the "I"-illusion. The "I"-illusion disappears in its absence.

Stay with this for a while, as it may just be revelatory. And, then, rest in the utterly self-forgetful stillness that allows the observation of the utterly self-referential chatter.

When we name, we give rise to "self" as well as to the appearance of objects of desire or aversion, the flip sides of craving. Name-and-form works to create not only an illusory sense of subjectivity but an illusory sense of an objective world.

We create the objects of our desire, aversion, or possessiveness. We, under the spell of ignorance and all the other conditions of dependent arising, do not see and know the objects as they are—imputed and illusory. Illusory objects can never quench desire—and yet we spend a great many of the precious finite moments of our life chasing them.

Another way to briefly get a sense of and some insight into the condition of name-and-form is to pause and commit to sit for a few minutes in inner silence. Sounds will arise in your environment. Watch your mind. Observe how it can't leave a sound alone, how it can't let a sound simply be a sound never heard before, never to be heard again in the same way. Note how the mind seeks to name it. That the mind seeks to name it is an impulse, an urge—the condition of craving that we will talk about in a bit.

Now we're watching name-and-form in action, as a creating force. Just observe this for a few minutes, watching what the patterned cycling of dependent arising's conditions does to the refuge of silence. Watch the universe name-and-form creates.

Whatever you decide the sound to be—that of a bird, a car, an appliance in the house, or a plane flying overhead—in the very naming, silence is broken. Note that self had not existed within silence.

With name-and-form breaking the silence, attention is grabbed instantly. Name-and-form is powerful. In a nanosecond, as name-and-form conditions the moment's arisings, it tumbles attention into a universe where not only does the thing we just named exist but "I," the namer, exist.

Naming, believing in label as more than simply convenience, is only one of the innumerable ways in which we fall back into the separate sense of self.

Silence is a refuge from self; self cannot enter silence. With the name applied, the silence is ended. This is name-and-form's creative force, creating in an instant both "self" and its inhabited universe of separate things. If this bird or car or appliance or plane exists, it exists within a universe where the separate sense of self also exists. If "bird," then "me."

IN HIS REALIZATION, Buddha offered a teaching on "specific conditionality": "Because of this, that arises."

This teaching appears—initially—as one of the most cryptic statements in the body of insights Buddha offered. It puzzles our conceptual mind. The very quality of being cryptic, the quality of having a hidden meaning, can invite our curiosity in. We recognize the statement as a hint and, as grace allows us the inclination, we can accept the invitation to explore, to inquire.

As we watch our own minds shaped and conditioned by the force of name-and-form at work, in very short order we can see the truth of the statement—"because of this, that arises"—in its elegant simplicity. Take a few minutes, if you will.

We posit one thing, giving it form through name. In doing so, we posit a universe of duality. Watch the labeling of the inner dialogue again for a bit, if you wish. Watch "label" impute an entire universe in which not only does the labeled appearance exist but "I" also exist. Watch "label" automatically impute "labeler." Because of this, that. Allow your whole being to take in the truth of what you've seen, allowing the realization to penetrate deeply. Our ideas about reality are not Reality.

"This" and "that" are fabrications, mere ideas. May we join mystic poet Rumi in his recognition that "out beyond all ideas ... there is a field." May we all meet on that field, a field always already present, far beyond the posited subjects and objects of name-and-form.

WE'VE MOVED THROUGH the first four links, or conditions, slowly. We've paced ourselves deliberately to explore and come to recognize the functioning of each condition in our own minds. We've taken the time to become acquainted with and to know for ourselves some of the conditions that allow "self" and the world of self to come into creation.

At times, the proliferation of the patterned dynamics proceeds slowly, as in the decades-long story of the birth, aging, and death of the individual with our nametag. Along with that snail-paced spin that only creepingly proliferates the cycle of suffering, there are always other spins of the wheel operating at a speed that is not at all slow or stately. Most "spins" operate in a blur behind the scenes. A new "I" is born, ages, and dies in endless quick spurts in every moment of our lives as the cycling simply whizzes along.

We will explore this dizzying pace as we see what happens after the stage is set for the "I"-illusion to make its starring appearance. We are constantly born anew. The Tibetan phrase for this dizzying pace—the fundamental nature of appearance in form—is *bok chuk*. This phrase is echoic, onomatopoeic—like *ba-boom, ba-boom, ba-boom*. It fires scenarios, creations, universes, and selves at the speed of an assault rifle. How foolish is our clinging.

Craving propels the whole system of suffering. The cycle of suffering has no other function but to produce and consume both experience and the experiencer: an endless, pointless, sorrowful game of Pac-Man. *Bok chuk*. We are run by our own projections.

If we were to hold name-and-form lightly, how quickly craving—the epitome of dualistic thinking—would simply cease. The illusion of separation would disappear in an instant and we would know ourselves as we are.

We would consciously abide in the grace from which we have never for a moment been separate—only "lightly dusted" with name-and-form.

15

The Six Senses

OUR SENSORY APPARATUS is the condition that allows and determines our apprehension. Apprehension is the faculty of understanding. It connotes perception on a direct and immediate level, an uncomplicated receptivity to information.

Our sensory apparatus includes our organs for sight, sound, touch, taste, scent, and—although not typically considered to be a sensory organ within a purely physical view—thought. The capacity to apprehend thought is that of the conceptual mind's. Conceptual mind is the apparatus, the sense organ, for our thoughts, mental operations, and mental images.

The six senses come with the territory of life-in-form; they are our biological equipment. This condition of the six senses functions as existential force—grounded in existing, arising simply from the experience of existing in a human body. We can think of the six senses as the precursors to perception. Perception occurs at contact. The six senses are our equipment for contact, the six "consciousnesses" we need for contact.

Buddha reminds us that "the whole of the world arises within this fathom-long body." If the world that arises is governed by ignorance and the laws of suffering that follow in its wake, that world is hell. If the world arises via wisdom's awakening trajectory, it is a "pure land," heaven on earth.

We will discuss the trajectory of awakening later. For now it is important for us to recognize, to see, how the condition of the six senses functions within the system of dependent arising.

In the system of suffering, the six senses allow for the provision of sensory data. Sensory data are the building blocks with which the complex feedback loops of karmic formations, name-and-form, consciousness, and ignorance create the world of appearances as it manifests to each of us. The contribution of the six senses further facilitates the apparent solidification of "self" and "other." The whole system works to continue self and the world of self—to keep the cycle ongoing and to keep attention bound within it.

When conditioned by as well as conditioning the other factors in the system of self and suffering, the six senses do not operate with the degree of naked awareness or neutrality of which they are capable. Like a flavor in a soup that has married with the other flavors, its functioning is affected by ignorance, karmic formations, consciousness, name-and-form, and the rest. All are in service to craving and craving's desire for becoming. Fueled by hope that the self *is* and that its cravings can and will be satisfied, we keep the cycle going.

We can pause, if you like, for a moment here, as it might be beneficial. Take some time to settle your mind. Be deliberate. Be grateful for the nobility of the practice you're engaging in. And, when your mind is somewhat still, your breathing perhaps somewhat free and easy, your sense of being relaxed, allow yourself to ask some questions.

What are the primary goals of my egoic sense of self? How do I keep trying to confirm its "real" and "true" existence? The questions do not have to do with achievement, accomplishment, or accumulation. They have to do with the most fundamental motivation of the egoic self-sense.

What evidence does the "I"-illusion seek for its existence? What confirmation will suffice?

We want to clearly see our attachment to the apparent continuity of the "I"-illusion. That attachment, self-grasping, runs the whole show. The egoic sense of self appropriates the innocent functioning of our senses, directing them to provide confirmation of its own assumed existence. It further distorts the mental faculty, leading to a confusion that is incapable of recognizing "I" as simply another thought, an idea, a mental image.

Clear seeing loses its footing within the unsteady confusion of samsara. Within ignorance and all of the other befogging conditions, we are incapable of seeing "I" as a distortion overlaid continuously upon each new moment. Just to recognize that, just to begin to discern that truth as we go throughout our day, is a blessing of enormous benefit.

WE CAN THINK of the six senses as six channels flooding the brain with information. As teenagers, my four kids would each be blasting different music from each of their rooms. I can attest that this is crazy-making. It's chaos. Amid even the normal daily bombardment of sensory data each of us experiences, the condition of consciousness leaps into play quickly. It tries to sort and make sense of the input in accordance with the imprints karmic formations have already laid down for information's gathering. It filters incoming data in homage to a predetermined coherence.

Memory—an interactive product of karmic formations and consciousness—plays a part here. It overlays past experience upon the present moment—and gives rise to a quick, facile recognition of familiarity. It dismisses the apprehension of freshness and uniqueness. Within the fog of ignorance, we rarely have a moment with a mindful and naked apprehension of sensory or conceptual arisings.

Within the distortion and self-reference of ignorance, the six senses no longer function simply as the building blocks of information and experience. The six senses begin to also function as the fields of potential pain we wish to avoid. They function as the fields where we seek pleasure. Seeking pleasant sensations is built into the confusion.

Sight, sound, taste, scent, touch, and thought are the territories we seek to choreograph, to manipulate, in an attempt to have them conform to our desires. Looking closely, we can see the conditioning effect of the six senses upon the condition of craving. Our desires manifest within the condition of craving. The six senses allow the appearance of the object of craving—or of aversion, which is craving in reverse—to appear.

We remain, conditioned as we are by ignorance, consciousness, karmic formations, and name-and-form, oblivious to the fact that we see, hear, taste, smell, touch, and think a tiny percentage of all that there is to see, hear, taste, smell, touch, and think. Our six senses have the capacity to apprehend only a sliver, a tiny fraction, of all that is. Yet, from their evidence, we posit a world existing exactly as we perceive it and conceive of it. In the fog—and indeed the complacency—of ignorance, we never pause to question our assumption. We stick to our guns.

Sit for a few minutes, if you wish, to simply pause and attend to the sensory input arising for you here and now. You will surely note impermanence.

Fleeting sound appearances, fleeting sensation appearances, fleeting thought appearances—all picked up by the radar of the six senses and formed by the conditioned, conditioning cycle of dependent arising.

Imagine that you just turned your six senses over temporarily to a visitor from another galaxy. As would the visitor, just listen. Just smell. Just sense the tactile experience. This is the sense data that we have in this moment.

Simply note the sense data without conceptual elaboration. Sit with at least a temporary willingness to surrender the habit or urge to elaborate. We can skip the color commentary of the ill-informed "talking head."

In Buddhism there is a phrase, "guarding the sense doors." It is a suggestion. I'll use the example of seeing to explain this phrase. The suggestion of guarding the sense doors points out that, when we are engaged in seeing, we focus on seeing. Instead of focusing upon the visual appearance—that which is seen—or upon the eye which is receiving the data of refracted light, we simply focus on seeing. We focus on the verb, not the noun. We focus on what is happening. In this case, seeing is happening.

Try this, if you like. Open your eyes and simply focus on seeing. Note that seeing is what is happening. You can try this with any of the six "sense doors." When we simply notice the seeing or the hearing or the tasting as what is happening, we are much less likely to react to that present moment's object of appearance. Sit and simply guard the sense doors for a while. With this simplicity, we can develop our ability to return to innocent awareness, free of conceptualization.

WE CAN REST in gratitude for the capacities of any or all of these six senses. These are our human gifts. Take the opportunity to experience deep gratitude for each of them in turn—for all that they have allowed us, for all the ways they have enriched us. Beauty brings us to our heart, and we would know far less of beauty without the six senses. They are precious gifts, enabling creativity, communication, and innocent contentment.

Hold the intention to use them with wisdom, to use them in service of awakening. Allow the intention to take root in your heart.

Rest at the very gates of the senses: the eyes, the ears, the nose, the tongue, the physical body, the capacity of conceptual mind. Deepen your insight into this condition of capacity. Deepen your insight into the formless awareness that allows these capacities to function. Rather than resting in that which is seen or heard, rest in that by which we can see, hear, smell, taste, touch, mentate.

Rest for a while in that awareness, free from elaboration.

16

Contact

THE CONDITION OF SIX SENSES is the condition of the existential capacity to apprehend an object of sight, sound, taste, scent, touch, or thought. Contact is the condition wherein the six senses actually apprehend the appearance. Contact is the condition of momentary connection of one of the six senses with a momentary arising in grace's endless display. Buddha pointed out that "with contact the world arises."

Contact, like our sensory apparatus, is a condition within the system of dependent arising that functions as an existential force. It comes with the territory of life-in-form and, in this way, certainly has survival benefit. We rarely recognize, however, that contact is conditioned by all of the forces operating within the system of dependent arising—in particular, by the conditions of karmic formations, name-and-form, craving, and grasping.

Contact arises in dependence upon a functioning sense organ, a functioning sense consciousness, and an object of apprehension. All three must be present. Contact arises in the moment of their interaction. It involves any phenomena known perceptually or through conceptual recognition. Contact is the moment an experience comes into attention. When contact arises without mindful attention, it confirms the separation that ignorance assumes.

Sit for a moment, if you like, and check this out in your own experience. If we're looking, we can recognize that we're looking with eyes that have the capacity to see, with a consciousness of seeing, and with an appearing object that reflects light back to the eyes—a visual appearance. In that moment, the other conditions of dependent origination link it with a mental image from the memories of karmic formations. Just sit for a bit, eyes wide open, and watch if this is so. Try it with hearing. We have organs capable of hearing, ear consciousness which can and does hear, and an object of the hearing—the appearance of the sound. Note how contact—the registering of the appearing sound—is quickly moved by the condition, *consciousness*, to link with a mental image from the memory banks of karmic formations.

It occurs with startling rapidity and carries attention along. We typically have no mindfulness that all of this is occurring within the formless awareness that allows the entire interaction, the formless awareness that contains the interaction as content. Remember, and rest for a bit, if you wish, within the formless awareness. Back away from the content and rest in that which contains it. Allow yourself to bathe in that clarity, to immerse your being in equanimity for a while. Equanimity, a gift of grace and an aspect of it, maintains balance and sanity regardless of the "content" of awareness.

EVERYTHING BEYOND the six senses and contact, beyond the raw data, is imagined. We imagine ourselves into samsara. When our attention is trapped in the cycle of suffering, we appropriate the raw data, bringing it into our narrative. We feed the ego through narrative.

Raw, impersonal data is personalized by ideas and memories and the powerful tendency of self-grasping. We have a conditioned blueprint of filtration and conditioned reactivity to what comes through it. The latter is the condition, *feeling*, at work. We'll look at that in a bit.

Karmic formations maintain a conditioned template—a stance, an ingrained and habitual organizational dynamic through which we experience life. Usually only data that makes sense within the frame of the template and/or stands out glaringly from it gets through to our active attention. Karmic formations place a veil over here and now, a veil that distorts. Think of how five people from different backgrounds give completely different accounts of what would seem to be the exact same event. In dependence upon innumerable saliencies and memories, we see what we believe and we believe what we see.

Think of any situation that arose in your day up until this moment and let yourself recall and visualize it in your mind's eye. What did you see? What do you understand of what you saw—how did you conceive of it? Ask one of the single most powerful questions there is to ask in any circumstance: What was looking—was this ignorance looking or wisdom looking?

Where is my attention placed as I look—in "self" or in grace? This question—in and of itself—has a powerful potential for awakening. I ask myself that question as often as I can remember to do so.

Contact provides the raw data of the present. When contact is tainted with self-reference, we do not simply register raw sensory data. We think the world into form. Typically, the experience of contact is contact with our idea of the object of contact rather than with its simple fleeting appearance. Attention is drawn into an arising idea. And the arising idea leads to a torrent of ideas that float attention helplessly away from here and now, as if carried along in floodwaters.

Ignorance views contact as an experience occurring with something "other" than "self." It does this via label, memory, and blind, habituated patterns. In so doing, we confirm ignorance in its imagined world of duality, of separation. We confirm the "I" we believe to be separate.

Buddhist teacher, Rodney Smith has pointed out that existence meets itself in contact. In contact, life meets life. Were ignorance not ever present when attention is trapped in the conditioned world of self and suffering, we would know that to be so in every newly arising moment. If we were to realize this truth—that existence meets itself in contact, that life meets life—our experience would be one of an unending stream of awe and wonder, of gratitude and compassion. We would recognize and trust and abide in grace.

There are several things to note about contact. First of all, contact does not multitask. It is selective. Out of innumerable visual or auditory or conceptual objects (thoughts or mental images) to which we could pay attention, we choose only a few. These few with which we actually make contact are chosen with self-reference and from within the deep trenches of egoic habits. Confirmation of opinion, novelty, annoyance, threat, and the slightest promise of the pleasure reward, for example, attract our attention. The condition of contact brings apparent form to the foreground. All else recedes to the sensory background during the moment of contact.

I remember one long night sitting up with a friend who had come to the end-stage of his terminal disease. That night, he was actively dying. Through the hours together, my eyes remained utterly focused on the rise and fall of his chest as he breathed the last of his finite number of breaths in this lifetime. I breathed with him—nothing more. Everything beyond the communion of our connected breathing simply fell away. Just before dawn, a member of his sangha came into the room.

The sangha member instantly removed a painting that was hanging on the wall above the dying man's pillow and replaced it with a Dharma book, per Tibetan tradition. I had not thought to notice the painting, the absence of a Dharma book, or to take the actions the dying man's other friend took. We attended to different things—I to the dying life before me and his sangha friend to what he considered to be the dying man's future lives. Different motivations, different moments of contact—different experiences.

There are plenty of people—people with a house full of buddhas or pictures of gurus on their altars or crosses in every room—for whom these artifacts cease serving as occasions of contact, cease serving as continual reminders of our desire to awaken. Often, they simply fade into the sensory background when other more compelling temporary urges arise. The urges pull attention out of our intention and into contact with a different agenda. I know this because I must often count myself in that "plenty of people" group.

Try an experiment, if you wish. Walk slowly around whatever environment you're in for a few minutes. There are a thousand opportunities for contact.

Look with mindfulness and note what appearances capture your attention. Note where your attention goes into the experience of contact, remembering that this contact also occurs with our own thoughts.

You might note the cascade of references and memories and assumptions as karmic formations condition the moment of contact. You might note an almost visceral feeling response to the experience of contact—either positive, negative, or indifferent—as the condition, *feeling,* comes into play.

Perhaps you'll notice name-and-form call attention into an appearance that had not stood out until that moment. Note the moment name gives form to an appearance—pulling it out from an immense spectrum of all that might be noticed. Note how name-and-form instantly reasserts the world *and* the "self" we believe in.

Note what attracts you. It will keep changing. Note where attention reaches out to make contact. No judgment, no elaboration—simply note. We're looking at all that can tumble attention back into ego. We're learning our own triggers.

Experiment with this, if you like. Pick up a stone or a similar small, hard object in the environment around you. Note the difference between the "I" who holds a stone, the "I" who makes contact with the object of awareness via touch consciousness—sensing—and the "I" who looks at a stone, the "I" making contact with the object of awareness via visual consciousness—seeing.

There are two utterly different experiences, each experienced by a different "I." And yet we, in both circumstances and both identities, apply both the label "stone" and the label "I." The condition, *consciousness*, quickly jumps in to coordinate the various sense consciousnesses into a single stream of "object" and a single stream of "me."

The point of the exercise is to deepen our awareness of the condition of contact at work in the ongoing creation of the cycle of samsara. Unmindful contact, as every other condition when operating unmindfully, propels the continued cycling of what Buddha called "the wheel of life and death."

So, if you wish, keep sitting and walking and making contact for a bit, and watch the tugs and drags upon attention. It's like mingling at a cocktail party. Notice where you like to mingle. Simply watch what's going on. We're looking into what has been operating our attention all this time, what has been endlessly spinning in our mindlessness.

ALL OF THE FACTORS of dependent arising come into play—they aggregate—around a moment of contact. They determine what catches our attention, what claims our notice. We can think of what is likely to still catch our attention, what are our remaining habitual tendencies in this regard. What opportunities are we likely to latch onto? Is it opportunity for pride or anger? For jealousy or disappointment? For discouragement? Is it opportunities for self-pity or self-aggrandizement? For what do I scan the horizon? No judgment, simply note. These are the habituated patterns of unhealed wounds that deserve both our attention and our compassion.

After having engaged in steadfast committed practice for however many months, years, or decades we've been practicing, we can notice the opportunities that we are likely to engage with have begun to change a bit. We can find ourselves more inclined to take advantage of an opportunity to practice patience with a difficult person. We can find ourselves more likely to reach out in greater compassion to another, recognizing that the very reaching out is healing and connecting and aligned with the truth of interbeing.

We can find ourselves much more self-forgetful. We begin to see that, as our self-reference diminishes, our sense of interbeing increases. With less self-reference, we are much more likely to allow the light of our individuality to come out in playfulness and love. We are much more present. Our relationship with contact becomes more awakened as we take everything less personally, as we hold more within an ever-increasing capacity to love, as we recognize the joy when existence meets itself in contact.

When I think of contact, I always think of the great elder Ram Dass. His point of reference, the determinant of his contact—all his contact—is that he is always talking to God. He shares that when he meets people. "I'm always talking to God. And, right now, God looks like you."

His insight is echoed in the beautiful realizations of Thomas Merton: "There is in all visible things an invisible fecundity, . . . a hidden wholeness. This mysterious Unity and Integrity is Wisdom. . . . There is in all things an inexhaustible sweetness and purity."

May we all transform the condition, *contact*, with mindful attention, and endlessly experience "inexhaustible sweetness and purity."

17

The Confluence of Conditions

IN THE MAKING OF A FILM, great attention is put into the gathering of props, the placement of props and players on the set, the lighting, the background music, the very nature of the film and camera, the angle of the camera, even the font used to announce the film's title. The phrase, mise-en-scène, refers to this gathering of conditions in service to the script, the ambiance that enables the telling of the story and the arising of the story's agent.

Let's pause for a moment and consider some of the implications of the conditions we've just been exploring.

Ignorance, karmic formations, consciousness, name-and-form, the six senses, and contact condition each other, as we've begun to see, in a patterning that brings a moment into form, that captures attention in a conditioned appearance. We will come to see, as we explore the next six conditions, how the called-forth appearance, arising at contact, calls forth an "I"-illusion.

Thomas Merton called the "I"-illusion "a radical falsity." Attention is seduced into that small, mistaken, bound experience of being. The conditions of dependent arising deepen attention's entrapment.

For the moment, sit for a bit, if you like, and simply watch the movements of your own mind as they recycle, over and over. Stepping back into a mindful, deliberate use of attention, see the interplay of the conditions of dependent arising. Without choreographing or strategizing or willing, simply note as you witness. What conditions do you recognize? Can you see their mutual conditioning? Take some time to name them if you can. Watch the collusion of their interplay.

Just spend a few minutes witnessing the mutual influence of conditions, the rise and fall of appearances to mind. Watch the thought "I" appear over and over—sometimes subtly, sometimes glaringly. Watch what led to its appearance. Watch where its appearance leads. Watch attention's habituated inclination to get trapped in it. Simply watch. Lean back and rest in the watching.

These are some of the operations of every unconscious moment, the dynamics that create and sustain the bound and illusory sense of self. When we thoroughly recognize the uneasy, energetic "frequency" of the "I"-illusion—that limitation and sense of separateness—our healthy yearning for a greater, deeper experience of being begins to carve out our shallowness and dilute our fears of surrender.

Just as grace has invited us, we begin to invite grace—and make room for—it.

A PENETRATING UNDERSTANDING of dependent arising has great liberative potential. The play of conditions is ongoing. If left unguarded by mindful attention, the whole system functions in varying time sequences simultaneously. *Bok chuk*, as we've discussed, is the Tibetan phrase used to describe the moment-by-moment creation and dissolution of fabrications. We can think of how we might snap our fingers in rapid succession—a few times in a row. This is how quickly the spinning wheel of dependent arising's conditions, creating samsara, can turn.

That sequencing of that spinning wheel can also turn more slowly, at the rate of a "chapter" in our lives—the movement from one significant egoic identification and another, or between one meaningfully transformative shift and the next. Think of the chapters in your life: the student to the graduate, the child to the parent, the promotion to the retirement, the beginning seeker to the mature practitioner. And the spinning wheel can turn at the rate of the entirety of our human life—from birth to death. The patterned conditioning remains the same at all speeds. The patterned conditioning is the schemata of suffering.

We can often see the patterned dynamics in hindsight, with a bit of what I call a "Dharma lag"—the time between an arising and our mindfulness of it. To catch the dynamics at their game—with the recognition that not only are they impersonal but that their very function is the creation of illusion—is to free trapped attention into the endless continuum of awareness. That continuum is an energetic "frequency" of sanity and wonder and peace—boundless.

Among countless other benefits, a daily practice cultivates the capacity to free attention, to employ it mindfully, to see. Pausing makes use of our developing capacity to see. In pausing, as we've come to recognize, we remove attention from the mindless rush. We need to be outside of the conditioned process to see it. As an informal practice throughout the day, pausing allows us to proclaim: "I once was blind but now I see."

When attention is trapped in ignorance, we lament with fourth-century Catholic mystic St. Augustine: "I sought where evil comes and there was no solution." With the honesty of the lament—his realization of the truth of suffering—he found grace or grace found him, just as grace has found us. Called by grace to practice, our hearts begin to open, to awaken. The capacity and willingness to pause, to see, and to surrender all take root. We begin to embody them. The "solution-less" sorrow of "evil"—the consequences of unmindful conditioned reactions—begins to release in realization, as do the reactive habits themselves.

Mystics in all traditions have long recognized that attention trapped in "self," in ignorance, has the consequence of suffering—both for the person whose attention is trapped and for those around him or her as the suffering spills over. Any contemplative or practitioner comes to recognize the difference between the fruits of "self" and the fruits of grace.

In Christian theological language, as Thomas Keating points out, there are clear realizations of "the three consequences of original sin." Original sin here can be understood as the mistaken assumptions that cast us from Eden. Nothing casts us from Eden except for our beliefs about existing as separate entities—separate from others, separate from all of creation, and separate from grace. These "three consequences of original sin" are *illusion* (not knowing what happiness is), *concupiscence* (looking for happiness in situations and objects that are incapable of offering genuine and stable happiness, such as objects of desire and lust), and *weakness of will* (the sense that we are so lost that we put forth no effort to be "found"). In Buddhism, this last illusion is recognized as "the laziness of discouragement." It arises from relying upon only the impoverished resources of "self."

Every wisdom tradition realizes the same truth. The contemporary Tibetan Buddhist Sogyal Rinpoche speaks of "original sin" in different language when he notes that "samsara arises as a result of...successive failures to recognize the essential nature."

The experience of a life felt as separate from the rest of existence is painful. It's a prison.

Buddha's teachings provide a view and method—a path—back to "original blessing." "Original blessing" is the blessing of our own essential nature, where we are always and already in union with the sacred, far beyond the limitations of "self."

EACH OF THE SIX CONDITIONS of dependent arising that we have already explored is, of course, conditioned by conditions we have yet to explore in any depth. And each of these first six conditions in turn conditions each of the other five. It is a dizzying play of forces and feedback loops.

Such a play of forces and feedback loops within a system such as this will produce a *harmonic*—a kind of emergent overtone. The harmonic of self is ever present within the system of dependently arising conditions. It's like the hum of conversation in a restaurant or of bees in a hive—the overtone of the conditions fabricating the present moment's appearance. We know that to be so as we begin to witness the hum of our own chronic self-reference in the midst of the flow of impersonal processes.

The desire for becoming someone is an aspect of karmic formations. The force of the six conditions we've explored harmonically resonate with that desire. They play upon it, in much the same way Himalayan "singing bowls," when played upon and vibrated in a certain way, produce a "singing" harmonic. Ignorance, karmic formations, consciousness, name-and-form, the six senses, and contact create the necessary conditions for the sense of self—the desire to become someone—to rise in tone and volume. They've set the stage, the mise-en-scène, for the "I"-illusion to appear as a blossoming and convincing mirage. They set world and "self"—and, inevitably, suffering—in motion.

Ignorance allows this cycle to continue unimpeded and unquestioned. Karmic formations, particularly the predisposition to establish a separate sense of self, shapes a sense of "entity"—"I" or "me"—rather than mere "process" on the entire cycle. Consciousness unifies data around that sense of self—"entity"—embroidering it with conceptual elaboration and creating the illusion of self's constancy.

Name-and-form creates form from formlessness, creating objects through name and imputing the fabricated objects as both separate and seemingly "known." Name-and-form labels the "entity" that ignorance and karmic formations impute upon the dynamics of these impersonal processes.

The six senses, conditioned by all other conditions, provide the raw data fueling the spinning cycle, creating and sustaining its illusions. As we've seen, the condition of contact, within this system of suffering, has its prejudices and filters. It has been conditioned not only by the six senses but by ignorance, karmic formations, consciousness, and name-and-form. Contact is the moment an experience comes into awareness. It whispers to the ever-present harmonic of self, calling attention to it as "experiencer" of the experience.

Sit for a moment again, if you like. Perhaps it will be helpful to take the condition that most resonated with you, the one you most clearly understood and recognized at work in your own mind. Check out how it conditions and is conditioned by the other five we've explored. Simply witness the dizzying interplay of just the first six of the conditions of dependent arising. Witness the stage set for all our suffering—our ever-present background of tension and malaise.

I can give an example in the hope that it is helpful. I was sitting outside early one morning, a beautiful peaceful morning. It was the kind of morning that invited gratitude and ease, that freely offered them. Suddenly, I found myself tense and anxious. Those states are well known to me, familiar. They're aspects of the karmic formations in my mind. Although I did not recognize the interplay of conditions instantly as they were arising—there was a "Dharma lag"—I realized within a few seconds that attention had turned away from the present to what the rest of the day could hold. The shape of the day was mine to decide; the day was free of obligation to anyone or anything.

Karmic formations, in the form of "oughts" and "shoulds" had arisen. Instantly, "I," the one who ought to, "I," the one who should, was named and formed. It captured my attention. The karmic habit of needing to fulfill the "oughts" and "shoulds" arose with the karmic formation of doubt about capacity to fulfill what ought and should be fulfilled. Anxiety was the result—*bok chuk*. David Whyte, the mystic poet, wisely points out that "there is a small opening into the new day that closes the moment you begin your plans."

Try witnessing another of the conditions in all of its relationships. Watch the thoughts and emotions in your own mind ricochet like balls in a quick game of pool. Observe your patterns. They are not who you are. Simply observe for a while.

And then take the time to rest in the awareness that is observing. Liberation lies in that sliver of distinction between a content of awareness and awareness itself.

WE CAN BREAK FREE from the entire attention-trapping cycle at any time by seeing through a single link, recognizing the power with which it has usurped attention. We can see it as an impersonal process producing an illusion of an entity. In so doing, we can reclaim our avenue into pure awareness.

There are skillful ways to work with each condition so as to free attention from the tangled web they all create. A single, oft-repeated question can help break ignorance's spell: What is looking right now—ignorance or wisdom? Is the experience foggy, complicated, confused, or is there a definitive, knowing clarity? Is attention looking from self or from grace? Is my "center of gravity" in my mind or in my heart? In the very asking of the question, we are applying the mindfulness that can see through and beyond the patterned cycling. We don't allow the "I"-illusion to take awareness's place.

Every last one of us has the capacity, as mystic poet John O'Donohue writes, "to reach beyond imitation and the wheel of repetition." Never doubt that capacity for "unbinding." Each of our individualities is a beloved manifestation of grace, never for a moment separate. Sit with that for a moment. Open to the meaning of the words. Let your heart gratefully resonate with them. Never doubt that grace is leading your awakening. No matter what's going on for each of us in this moment, *this*—exactly *this*—is what our own awakening looks like.

Karmic formations loses its power to determine our experience and our reactions when we recognize habitual pattern arising. Recognizing it, we know it to be ingrained and familiar. We can increasingly recognize it with a lightness that already acknowledges, "I am not my habits of body, speech, and mind." We can get the hijacker out of the pilot's seat. Again, it is mindful attention that allows us to unbind in each single instance of recognition.

Each single instance of recognition of habit and release of attention that had been bound within it weakens the power of the entire system of suffering. Every moment of recognition weakens its hold. Not a single one of those moments is wasted. We can practice throughout the day in this way. It is in our formal practice, though, with silent and unmoving attention, that we have the capacity to burn away its power once and for all.

The condition of consciousness—our quick jump to conclusions and a glib cohesive story—can be recognized in a pause, such as the pauses we've engaged in so many times throughout this discussion. Pauses have power. When deliberately engaged in, they stop the momentum. It's like poking a stick in the spokes of a spinning wheel. It brings the cycling to a halt.

We can recognize name-and-form as it arises and recognize how conditioned it is by all the other conditions. Although labeling is useful and convenient, we get bound in the unconscious patterning of dependent arising when we fail to see the veil of illusion name-and-form imposes upon an arising. That veil obscures the freshness of the moment. We miss grace's newest unfolding.

With labeling—and this is perhaps its most covert danger—we impose upon mere fleeting appearance the imputation of solid, enduring, and separate existence, existence from its own side. That is precisely the illusion—taking mere appearance to be inherent existence.

It is, again, not that appearances don't exist. They don't exist in the way that we, in mistaken conception, think they exist. We saw that a while back when we inquired into what it is to see "my hand."

When we begin to recognize this and practice throughout the day within this recognition, a new freedom begins to flourish as well as a deep sense of holy responsibility in the living of our lives. Although it may appear paradoxical to ordinary conceptual mind, freedom and kindness arise and grow together. Freedom manifests in kindness. Conversely, kindness grows freedom.

Each time we recognize name-and-form at work, we have an opportunity to accomplish two things. We can meet our responsibilities in "conventional reality" through the label. And, we can recognize the profound mystery of the way things exist beyond the label. We can come to recognize "label" as having no more substantiality than a thought. When we do this with the label, "I," our human nature and our Buddha nature can begin to merge.

LET'S LOOK at two conditions together: *the six senses* and *contact*. Unmindfully, the two conditions can carry attention along in the cycle of self and suffering. We can arrest the cycle's momentum with the simple, time-honored act of "resting at the sense gates." This means that we simply note "seeing," for example, when experiencing a visual appearance. We take the focus off the "I" who is seeing, the eye that is receiving the refracted light, and the appearance of the seen. We rest in the verb. "Seeing, seeing, seeing." We skip the nouns. The verb is all that is happening.

And be chill about it. You wouldn't even be moved to wonder, explore, and inquire in these ways if grace weren't already waking you up. May we all grow in that trust. It makes life so much easier. In a beautiful phrase from a Tibetan prayer, we are "fortunate beings seeking great enlightenment." And—awakening beings, all—we are led by grace every step of the way.

Since we don't typically witness our minds with continual mindfulness, the cycle of suffering often continues for most of us, although certainly—as we remain steadfast in our practice—to a lesser and lesser degree. We'll turn next to what happens when the whole rolling, entrapping web is allowed to proliferate. It binds attention ever more deeply.

As we explore the next six conditions in turn, we will see the "I"-illusion pop on the stage that the first six conditions has prepared. We'll see it strengthen in its sense of vividness and reality, oblivious to its deceptive and insubstantial underpinnings. We'll see it, fueled by mindlessness, ready to alight and feed upon any one of a thousand fleeting thoughts, feelings, and appearances.

Contemplating the next six conditions of dependent arising, examining the force of them within our own minds, we'll see the dynamics of hunger for becoming. We'll witness the dynamics as they seemingly feed that self-sense within the confusion of the confining, vibrating web of conditions. And we will come to trust that simply and clearly seeing any one of the conditions will break the spell of this old, uncomfortable, and binding trance. Clear seeing is a path to grace.

PART FOUR

Fools Rush In

18

Feeling

OUR DISCUSSIONS AND CONTEMPLATIONS thus far have brought us through the exploration of the "ground environment," set by ignorance and inhabited by the next five links in the system. These are the conditions that set the stage for the arising of self and suffering. We've explored to the point of contact, the arising of an experience of apprehension. As grace continuously unfolds sense objects, the interaction of the sense organs with those objects results in seeing, hearing, smelling, tasting, touching and sensing, or thinking. Each interaction comes with emotional kite tails, from subtle to blatant.

We'll turn now to look at and contemplate the powerful seduction of *becoming* that begins its voracious and mushrooming escalation with the experience of contact.

Upon contact, feeling arises. It is the first conditioned reference, conditioned psychic orientation, placed upon an experience. Feeling—as a condition of the entire patterned interplay of dependent arising—does not here refer to emotion or emotionality as we typically think of it and experience it.

Angry, discouraged, jealous, and sad, for example, are emotions. They are not the referent here. *Vedanā* is the word used in Sanskrit to help distinguish this particular condition, *feeling*, from our habituated "feelings" or emotions with which, unmindfully, we usually always identify. Without wisdom, we adopt one of two inconsistent relationships with our emotions. On one hand, we believe that we own them. On the other hand, we allow them to own us and often acquiesce to their powerful lead.

Emotions are the physiological reaction to "charged" thoughts about self, others, stories, and circumstances. Think of fear and its energetic impact on the mindbody. Think of grief. Emotions are an energetically weighted, habituated response of the whole being. Aware that there is a learning curve, we can trust that it is within our capacity to work with emotions consciously, directing their powerful energy in the service of awakening.

Feeling, in the context of dependent arising, is far more subtle and elusive than our emotions. It takes some time for us to catch feeling with its hand in the cookie jar.

Feeling arises upon contact in every moment of contact. In every moment of contact, each experience has a conditioned inclination, a leaning toward a particular disposition. Feeling arises with one of three characteristics—positive, negative, or indifferent (neither-positive-nor-negative). Feeling arises subtly, fleetingly, minimally. Yet it can have powerful potentiality. It can pull attention back from its natural resting place in pure awareness and into the system of self and suffering. It can lead to unconsidered, unconscious action.

Positive feeling in reaction to contact holds the seed of desirous attachment. We all know what egoic mind is capable of when under the sway of desirous attachment. We can think of all the finite, precious moments of our lives we've squandered in chase of lust or reputation or even objects. We can think of the harm we've brought down on ourselves and others in the name of greed or pride or comfort.

Negative feeling upon contact holds the seed that, if watered, gives rise to a toxic continuum spanning the spectrum from the mildest twinge of disappointment to aversion to murderous rage. Our hearts begin to harden the moment it arises, no matter how subtly. Negative feeling arises as an energetic contraction.

Indifference, the third possibility for the condition of feeling, is not equanimity. Equanimity is a higher-order quality, a noble quality. It is free from personal reactivity and has the capacity to fully understand and remain fully open to what is arising. Indifference is a personal reactivity lacking both understanding and openness.

Indifferent feeling as a reaction to contact—also called *neither-positive-nor-negative*—holds the seed of continued ignorance. It perpetuates ignorance in the sense that indifference ignores. The feeling of indifference holds, as well, the suffering inherent in a continued sense of seeming separation. We pay no regard to that toward which we feel indifferent. The feeling of neither-positive-nor-negative holds the seeds of an uncaring lack of involvement and engagement. Think of the tens of thousands of beings we encounter in a lifetime, either via physical presence or via the media, for whom contact is registered as indifferent. As awakening beings, we have to examine how small or large, how inclusive or exclusive, is our circle of caring.

We can ask ourselves how close does someone have to be to my sense of "I" and "me" and "mine" to include that being in my care? With such an inquiry, we can witness where we are not yet connected, where there are blind spots in our understanding of our interbeing in grace. When we witness our lack of caring—whether it be in relationship to others or to the planet—we are observing ignorance. The wisdom observing the ignorance *already* cares. Wisdom and compassion are facets of the same precious jewel, the jewel of awakened mind.

It is beneficial to learn to recognize the arising of feeling upon contact since it is one of those conditions, like karmic formations, that functions with a determining force. Feeling funnels in all the conditioning dynamics and, particularly with a lack of mindfulness, determines the trajectory of the movement. Feeling can determine the arising of the next moment in lockstep accordance with its knee-jerk reactivity. It functions as a force that tightens and constricts, limiting endless potentiality and rushing it toward a contracted, predetermined arising.

Feeling tantalizes our habits of mind and our desire for becoming someone. It dangles a landing field for the "I"-illusion, a "me" with history, a "me" with hunger. Feeling is an advertisement, a bait thrown in the water of attention. We would do well to detect its "here, little fishy" call.

DETECTING THE CONDITION of feeling at play requires a pause that allows illumination, a pause that allows us to shine a light on what's going on. My suggestion here and now is to simply sit where you're at—and notice.

Do a simple body scan, slowly noting the sensations that arise as you move attention methodically from the top of your head all the way down to the tips of your toes. Simply scan; simply observe physical sensations. Look with subtle attention at each feeling arising upon each moment of contact. You will note, also, thoughts related to your physicality. Note the reaction of feeling to each new appearance to mind. There are only three things to note about feeling. It's only either positive, negative, or neither-positive-nor-negative (indifferent.)

Pay attention to the feeling that arises with each physical sensation that attention notes. What is the feeling upon noticing an ache or an itch or a tension in the musculature? What is the feeling upon noticing a catch in our breath or upon noticing increasingly relaxed breathing? Is it slightly positive? Slightly negative? Is it neither—indifferent?

You may notice, as you're scanning physical sensations, that you're noting through the medium of a mental image you have of your body, an inner template of its parts, the locations of the parts, and its presumed boundary. Note the feeling that arises upon contact with any mental image of your body that appears. Particularly in our body-conscious culture, mental images of our various parts and areas of our body can elicit a strong feeling reaction.

Note arising thoughts and check the instantaneous subtle feeling reaction arising with each moment of contact with a thought, a memory, an anticipation. Learn to pay attention to feeling. It can lead us off the trajectory of our longing to awaken and down a long detour.

THE CONDITION, *feeling*, can pull us into pain and trap us in confusion. The more lost we are in ignorance, bound in identification with the separate eddy, the more we find ourselves subject to and at the mercy of feeling. We're vulnerable to the mushrooming rush of grasping, craving, becoming, and birth—landing right back in aging-and-death (suffering) as we have so many times before. The more lost we are in ignorance, the more we careen out of control with feeling—even if that careening doesn't appear wild, even if that careening appears as just another life of "quiet desperation."

Recognizing the condition, *feeling*, we can see that much of our life has been spent in relation to our emotions and thoughts about life rather than *in* life. Without mindful attention, all of the conditions of dependent arising keep us in an imagined relationship with life.

There will never be contentment for as long as that is so. An imagined relationship offers no sustenance. We need to stay attuned to the subtle cues of feeling. Attentive, we can watch these cues light up the stage, indicating the next act of imagination is about to unfold.

In pausing, we can see exactly how it is that attention gets so lost in these illusions. With mindfulness, we can watch the illusion of "self" brought into being.

We simply observe the movements of the conditions within our own mind. We can see, as we observe feeling arise upon an experience, that the experience is simply an experience—nothing more. The experience does not induce the feeling. The entire conditioned system of self and suffering induces the feeling.

We can notice, too, that although thoughts of separation and duality have been present as part of the ground environment or stage set all along, feeling is the first energetic experience of duality. Energetically, an experience of a "wedge" arises, a reinforcement of the assumption of separating space between "me" and "not me." The misconception is that "I," identifying with feeling, am other than the object I mistakenly believe is causing the feeling.

With the condition of feeling in and of itself, there's still no "I." There's just inclination, a slight predilection to lean a certain way. Although it's elusive, we can increase our mindfulness of the conditioning influence of feeling. It's our early warning system—if we are mindful—that spaciousness is about to be narrowed, that "self" is about to intensify, that habituated agendas are about to follow their own conditioned imperatives.

None of this is personal. None of this is who we are. This is ignorance, an utterly impersonal dynamic, at work. We want to invite inquiry into that ignorance; we want to invite grace.

Increased mindfulness engenders growing confidence.

Unbinding—freeing attention from this great mass of suffering—is possible for all of us.

19

Craving

THE SIX "STAGE-SETTING" conditions we've explored function to funnel infinite possibility through the vortex of feeling. Feeling is a tiny elusive sliver of conditioned reaction to an appearance that arises in dependence upon those very conditions. From the moment the condition, *feeling*, weighs in on the arising appearance, there is a propensity to rush toward craving, toward a self that craves and hopes to grasp. When feeling weighs in, momentum can begin to build toward becoming "someone."

Craving is a proliferating force in the cycle of dependent arising. It accelerates the spin of the wheel of ignorance, impelling attention forward in the name of desire. Craving propels and begins to compel the potentiality of the harmonic of "I" to be pulled into appearance.

Craving is a beginning whine, an incipient insistence of an urge. In dependence upon the intensity of feeling arising in reactivity to contact, the object of contact and our history with it (karmic formations), the consciousness that quickly jumps to assumptions, and the ignorance that allows the unhelpful game to continue, craving asserts itself. It's been set in motion.

Conditioned by salience and history, mood and meaning, craving can pounce upon a feeling and exaggerate feeling's reaction. Craving's exaggeration of the feeling lights center stage, inviting wanting (or not wanting) to appear. It provides the platform where the sense of self can, in short order, alight. It offers a personalized invitation to the "I"-illusion.

Craving quickly moves the moment's dynamic from one of simply noticing a contact to an appearance—mental or physical—to one of grabbing our attention. One of my children, when her young self did not feel she had my full attention, would put a hand on each side of my face and literally spin my head toward her. Craving is like that. It turns our head and seizes our attention. Craving captures our attention, holding it and pinning it on the appearance and our reaction to it, whether that reaction is one of clinging or aversion. Clinging and aversion are two sides of the same coin.

One phrase used in Buddhism to describe craving's function is "*inappropriate* attention." With inappropriate attention, the object of our attention—whether of desire or antipathy—looms larger than life, pushing all else out of the mind. It fills the screen of the mind.

My most flagrant example of inappropriate attention involved a child, a sofa, and the Fourth of July. As a single mother I had very little to spare but, over the course of a year or two, was finally able to save enough to buy our very first new sofa. My kids and I moved it into place in the living room, stood and admired it, and then sat down and cuddled up, enjoying it. I went off to work the next morning happy and grateful. When I got home one of my daughters met me at the door—with great tears of contrition—and confessed that she and her friend, in a Fourth of July spirit, tried to make "sparklers." Sitting on the couch that afternoon, they twisted pieces of paper towels, lit the tips, waved them around, and watched the sparkles. Every single one of the sparkles left a tiny burn mark on the brand new sofa. There were hundreds of them.

Although we lived on a beautiful harbor—a view from each window—every time I walked through the living room for the next many months, I didn't even notice the water or the sunlight or the boats. My head turned instantly to the sofa, and all I saw were the burn marks. My eyes riveted on them. My attention was held hostage, grabbed by the intensity of my reactivity, calling me into frustration and self-pity and away from beauty and ten thousand new moments—inappropriate attention in action! Months later, December found my inappropriate attention still trapped in July.

With close inspection, we can see that craving is not so much about the triggering appearance. Craving is our reaction to the appearance. Our reaction is one of unmet desire; it is unsettling. The urge is to seek the satisfaction of having the unsettling energy of desire cease.

This condition, craving, operating under the auspices of ignorance, is deeply confused. It mistakenly posits duality, seeming to confirm a world split in two—"I" and what "I want" or "don't want." It deepens the ignorance that is its originating condition. It more deeply ingrains our belief that our mental images, our fabrications—including the craving "self"—have substance, have a reality.

In ignorance we quickly come to view the seemingly separate object as something that might satisfy the growing presence of urge—whether the urge be to have what we want and grab on to it or to not want what we have and push it away. Full wanting is an imperative, a "must." Full wanting is grasping, the next condition. This condition, craving, is incipient wanting, not yet precisely articulated, not yet insistently an imperative but an unsettling, unmet urge seeking momentary respite.

That distinction is important. Craving is experienced as *an arising condition*—in capitals, in bold letters, underlined. It is a useful red flag for our mindful attention. Since it is a bit less insistent and urgent and fixated than grasping, craving allows the possibility for a quieted mind—a mind that has paused to see—to simply witness it. In other words, we still have a fighting chance to keep from getting carried away in the force of grasping. With the willingness to forsake craving's desire, to simply ride the urge out, we renounce the next formation of "me," the next experience of dukkha.

WE CAN ASK OURSELVES how this dynamic plays out in our own minds. What are our habitual objects of desire? Our habitual objects of aversion? We can observe our confused desire at work. If the form of the appearance is one we hold with incipient attachment—such as praise, a new car, a person who strikes us as attractive, or the last spoonful of ice cream—we equate the acquisition of the desired object with the fulfillment of the escalating urge. We lean in the direction of *grabbing onto*. Conversely, if the form of the appearance is one we hold with incipient aversion—such as a difficult person, an insult, or rejection— we equate the destruction or avoidance of the object of aversion with fulfillment of aversion's urge. We lean in the direction of *pushing away*.

In either case, when we see clearly we can recognize that what we are really attempting in our actions is the quieting of the disturbing stage of impulse, the disturbing mind of utterly trapped attention. The energetic force of craving threatens our comfort. It is our reaction that seeks the satisfaction of having its unsettling energy cease. Comfort is mindlessness's favorite location.

CRAVING CAUSES A MOMENTUM, a wave of impulse—all the painful habitual addictions of ignorance, colored by memory. The most powerful addiction is to ego, to becoming someone.

It is painful to look and recognize our habits and urges—our greed, our pride, our vengefulness. We certainly resist it and certainly wish there were an easier way to our essential nature than the passage through brutally honest self-reflection. But we need to look—grace calls upon us to look—if we wish to awaken. Awakening *is* looking. Martin Laird notes that "we become aware of the mental habits . . . not because we are moving into darkness . . . but because of our increasing proximity to . . . very loving light." We are illuminated in looking and we are freed in seeing.

Craving flourishes in ignorance, in unmindfulness. It is the ever-ready chauffeur for our frivolousness and our assumptions. We can think of thousands of times we mindlessly went to the refrigerator or dialed a friend or checked our email, for example. At the extreme, we can think of the disturbed young men who eye their targets and their guns as the craving builds up and grasping takes over, and they walk into an elementary school or an Orlando nightclub. Operating without mindfulness, craving runs the gamut from seemingly inconsequential to profoundly consequential actions.

Craving arises as an escalating urge and can transport us quickly into compulsion—the condition of grasping. Nisargadatta's observation of the power inherent here is that "desire is the memory of pleasure and fear is the memory of pain." All of our craving and grasping is in response to our own mental images.

Pause for a moment, if you would, and review your actions of the past few hours. What bit of gossip or daydream, memory or hope, grabbed your attention? What did you reach for? What did you push away? What did you want? What did you not want?

Just note. Craving is a universal condition. It arises and manifests in each of us in certain shared ways as well as in uniquely individual ways, according to our history and karmic formations. Simply note. Whatever it is that you note, just recognize that these are the triggers that grab your attention out of peace, out of equanimity, and pull it back into the "I"-illusion, an "I" with an urge.

In this pausing that allows us to see, we're simply illuminating how enslaved and bound we are within our habits and urges. We're illuminating the first noble truth. Our own realization of that truth—a deep and direct realization in our own being—is key to freeing our bound attention.

Buddha described the entire cycle of dependent arising, an endless continuity of consequence, in human terms—in terms of thirst and hunger. The condition of feeling, it could be said, whets the appetite. Appetite is aroused in the condition of craving. Very simply, appetite is wanting—or its flip side, not wanting. Appetite is the wish for things to be other than they are in that moment.

The progression of the quick movement of conditioned and conditioning arisings leading to the condition of craving could be compared to all the preparatory, behind-the-scenes work done by others in a kitchen. We've all had that experience. Sitting in another room, our attention is caught when wonderful scents begin to drift out into the house. The feeling arising upon contact with the aroma of cinnamon and apples, for example, is positive (for most of us, anyway!).

Attention has been caught in the contact, and the condition of feeling is the seed of appetite. Craving raises its potency at this point, fed by the interplay of the other conditions. Craving *is* appetite, the beginning of caricature and exaggeration—reactivities that cause emotions to leap to their feet.

Craving reacts to an idea of an object, imputing the object as separate and external, believing in the reality name-and-form gave label to. It can lead us to seek its fulfillment in something as innocent as the taste of apple pie. It can lead us to seek its fulfillment in harmful actions—in rage, abuse, callous indifference, dishonesty, disrespect— the whole host of ignorance's demons.

If we pause to recall an incident of craving—perhaps a recent one, perhaps a deeply ingrained one that controlled the narrative and direction of our life for a long while—we can see the dynamics and consequences of craving's continuous re-creation. Just observe a recollection of a craving. We can ask ourselves, what is the experience craving wants? What are the resolutions it seeks? What does it hope for? What are the beliefs contained in the craving?

We want to simply note our own habituated inclinations. If we pause long enough with intention, we allow wisdom to discern what dictates craving adheres to, what sense of incompletion craving seeks to fill.

Craving reacts to itself—its own wanting or not wanting. It functions as a force demanding its own satiation. These patterned dynamics leave us, when unmindful, at their mercy. Craving is an unscratched itch demanding its fulfillment, a sense of deficiency yearning for completion.

Craving is our greed, the epitome of self-cherishing. Greed preys upon greed. It is our own greed that is the target of the greed of others in an elaborate pecking order creating inequity, injustice, and environmental harm. It is and always has been the cause of millions of the world's tribulations.

Sit, if you would, for a few minutes in silence, ingathering your attention. Take some time for a short meditation. Begin with an intention to see, to witness. Plant the intention firmly in your being, as if it were a flag laying claim to a new world. Take refuge in ever-present grace.

You can choose an object of meditation, such as a mantra or the sensation of the breath or you can choose to engage in objectless meditation as in Centering Prayer. In either case, observe what arises. Note the moments of mental stability, where attention—however brief or sustained—remains still and unwavering. Note what impulses pull your attention away from your intention. Note the undertow of thought and other mental habits.

Note the experience of craving. Notice how it pulls attention back into the system of suffering. I would imagine each of us knows the seductions: "I'll come back to meditation in a moment—I just want to think this thought a little longer," for example. It's a pull, as is every pull into past or future, out of here and now. Our experience of craving is of an urge, of temptation, of being lured. There's an old joke that our parents know how to push our buttons because they're the ones who put them there. In the same vein, the conditions of dependent arising have a rutted familiarity with what will work to capture our attention and will use anything as bait. We salivate.

In this contemplative pause, we note when mental stability is disturbed. Note the urge attempting to pull attention away. Note the undertow. Lack of mindfulness is a dangerous ocean, an ocean of samsara.

As often as it arises, note the escalating urge—this is craving. Become familiar with the escalating urge. Become familiar with craving. Pain and confusion—the entire cycle of self and suffering—drive this condition, just as craving refuels the entire cycle. It is restless and driven, at times caught in hopelessness, at times caught in acts of callous and indifferent harm. It arises from the inner poverty we experience when we rest in separateness, as an eddy, bereft of grace.

The courage necessary to remain unmoved, to remain in stability, in the face of craving comes to us through the wisdom and equanimity of clearly seeing what is so.

Seeing what is so is grace's gift to us. It strengthens as attention becomes unbound.

Respect yourself in the course of this brief meditation for the willingness to illuminate and stare down craving, and for the courage to stand firm in the face of it. This is possible only with mindful attention. With mindful attention, perspective shifts. The craving that had seemed so much larger and more powerful than who we thought we were is revealed, through wisdom's eyes, to be infinitely smaller, infinitely less powerful than the formless awareness observing it.

Rest in respect and gratitude for grace's gift of mindfulness.

Rest in respect for the growing sincerity and empowerment of your intention to awaken.

20

Grasping

LET'S TURN OUR ATTENTION NOW to the condition of *grasping*. To recognize it at work in our own minds is to recognize attention's most dangerous hijacker. Under the cover of ignorance, it can move quickly to full-blown power, taking total control of our attention.

Aware of growing urge, of craving, functioning in our own minds, we can learn to ride the temporary waves of its discomfort, the unsettling and insistent tug its lack of satisfaction exerts. We can grow in our capacity to simply observe it as a content of awareness. We can grow in our capacity to discern its habituated force and to recognize it as "not me," as simply an arising impersonal condition. Such discernment and recognition can release attention and identification held within it so that it no longer holds us hostage, holds us bound.

Should the condition of craving proceed without being either noticed or recognized as an indication of another strand in samsara's web, the whetted appetite of the urge can quickly rise in volume. The system of self and suffering begins to move more swiftly here, as the forces of the conditions amplify. It's like the rapid spinning of water in a vortex as it runs down the drain. The dynamic allows the condition of grasping to step forward in delight, grab hands with the want, and proceed unimpeded.

All of this typically occurs in a blur, an intricately spinning set of conditions that has processed and produced the "I"-illusion innumerable times.

We are looking now at how the impulse conditioned by craving rapidly morphs into grasping. The calling card of grasping is focused intent or "wanting." Craving, an itchy urge, moves to grasping, a strong, desirous want. The dynamic creates an opportunity for the sense of self to begin to coalesce, to begin to move into the next condition, *becoming*. "Wanting" demands a "wanter." Grasping offers wanting the chance to become personalized.

"I" is an emergent here, an overtone of the buzz of desire, increasing in volume and a sense of urgency. The emergent "I" senses a place to alight, to feed itself into becoming. When we clearly witness this for ourselves, as it plays out in our own minds, there is the shocking recognition that we're watching our mind chasing after its own thoughts. The location of the desire is at the idea, the mental image of the "want."

In the condition of grasping, the thought "I" begins to connect with the urge "want." The separate sense of self begins to arise with a charged vividness. The thought of "I," is of course present in all of the conditions, although often nascent, implied, assumed. The impulse to claim "I" is the condition of grasping. Although it may appear that the object of grasping is something external to "self," the primary object of grasping is the sense of "I."

We can recognize the compulsion to grasp *for* when we can see aspects of ourself in the greedy kid pushing the other trick-or-treaters out of the way to grab the biggest handful of candy. We can recognize the compulsion of aversion when we notice ourselves striking back doubly hard at a perceived insult (or at least picturing it in our minds.) Both forms of the impulse feed the "I"-illusion.

Craving is the initial appearance of a pull toward wanting. Grasping begins the identification with want: the "I" who is wanting, the "I" who wants. The vividly charged sense of "I" is believed. It seems—as experienced—to be real, substantial, and a defining locus of identification. The whole system of self and suffering moves to compel attention in this way.

The identification of the "I" who wants seizes on the opportunity to satiate and reduce the hungering discomfort of the urge. Ignorance allows the assumption that this satiation is necessary, will be permanent, and that the fabrication to which we're reacting with either attachment or aversion actually has the power to satisfy the compulsion.

We know from behavioral psychology that the reinforcement or conditioning schedule with the longest-lasting effects is one of random, intermittent reward. And each of us has had the "good moments," that satisfy, at least temporarily, the strong, pleasure-seeking focus of our unconscious motivations. They keep us going. Abandoning mindful attention and whatever wisdom we have, we just keep pushing the reward lever—whatever that might look like for each of us based on the latent tendencies of karmic formation. We hope each new push will be the push that will bring the pleasure. We forget that even our "feel good" moments are impermanent and inextricably linked to the cycle of suffering. We forget that each spin of the wheel spins us away from grace.

Grasping is powerful. It is the penultimate proliferating force in the cycle of samsara—a cycle propelled by desire arising within ignorance. In Tibetan Buddhism, this compulsion that grabs attention and clenches attention in its teeth is called *shenpa*. Roughly translated, it means "hook." The rapidity with which it plunges attention into the conditions of becoming, birth, aging-and-death (suffering) can be stunning.

The sense of "I," existing only as harmonic, becomes a believed thought with which attention makes contact. The "I"-illusion is brought into the foreground. Grasping is a frenetic, personalized mind of compulsion.

Two things seek satisfaction in grasping. One is the frenetic wanting of a release from the discomfort of urge. The second is self's need for becoming. Much of the time, this happens so quickly and so unconsciously that we have no awareness of it whatsoever. Much of the time, we are only aware of grasping when it is charged and intense. Picture a situation where you might be falsely accused of stealing someone's money, for example. The grasping to prove ourselves innocent would be fairly easy to observe. With mindfulness, we grow increasingly able to catch the dynamic at work in increasingly subtle manifestations. As we grow in our capacity to mindfully open to the experience of grasping, we grow in our capacity to resist the felt need to satisfy it. A stable, ingathered mind of inquiry is stronger than the compulsion.

Blindly following grasping is changing suffering. It mires attention more deeply in samsara. We acquiesce to ignorance in our assent to the notion that "I" exist and that my desires can be satisfied by fabrications. Grasping feeds self and suffering.

This is not to say that we can't eat a brownie or have sex or buy a new car, if we choose. We can enjoy any one of these with gratitude, fully aware of the temporality of the pleasure. There is a world of difference between grasping and enjoyment. Conscious, mindful choice allows enjoyment, without illusion or deeper binding. Enjoyment is simply grateful. Gratitude, when full and thorough, leaves no room for self—it's empty of self.

TO GET A SENSE OF GRASPING, we can look at our attachments. Each compulsion has deep roots in our survival imperative. We can look at the desirous attachments that keep us bound. We can look at what it is that we're unwilling to surrender about this illusory sense of self.

Sit for a while with this, if you like, in honest self-reflection. Look at your egoic attachments. Look at your aversions.

Do they exist in relation to objects, to people, to recognition, to a certain overlay of order? We can ask, am I attached to "being right" or to illusions of security? Am I attached to being liked or respected or in control? Am I attached to certain self-images? What do I name as the necessary conditions for my comfort? What "deprivations" could I not bear?

Along this line of inquiry, Buddha suggested we look at "the eight worldly concerns." These "concerns," to which each of us has conditioned reactivity are: loss and gain, pleasure and pain, fame and blame, praise and shame. Even saying the words silently to ourselves can evoke our own habituated reactions.

Staying with this inquiry, we can begin to recognize that grasping manifests as the neediness experienced by a tenuous sense of separate self. We can ask, what props and crutches does my ego believe to be—and experience as—necessary? Where do I turn when they are not available?

Observing this closely, inquiring into it, we come to clearly recognize grasping as a compulsion. It is a compulsion to satisfy the urge, arisen with craving, around which the "I"-illusion has localized. Without an understanding of the nature of the self or of the nature of suffering, we will remain as lost and bound as we've ever been in grasping. We can ask, what has led me all this time?

This exercise can be humbling. Open to what's humbling. Open to humility. Humility clears out the space that pretension, assumption, and attachment have taken up for a long, long time.

Genuine humility gives rises to compassion. It softens our hearts.

If you like, take the last few minutes to rest in compassion for yourself and for all of us so often lost in the pervasive, tense unease of samsara.

21

Becoming

HAVING COME TO RECOGNIZE craving in our own minds, we can identify it as the condition where "fools rush in." Craving begins with the inclination to act and react in accordance with whatever feeling arises upon contact with an appearance. There is a slight sense of ownership or identification at this juncture of feeling. Exaggerating feeling, craving calls to the "I"-illusion, offering a potential place to land.

We know that pausing and simply inquiring into what's actually going on here at this turn in the wheel of suffering can free us from its spell. We can pull back the exaggeration, quiet the emotionality and the stories that justify the reactivity, and simply see the dynamics. Although they are familiar, with mindful attention we see that they are blind and impersonal. Stepping into wisdom, we can step out of suffering and the trance of "self."

We've also, through our inquiry and contemplation, recognized grasping. We've observed it operating in our own minds when it's unmindfully allowed and implicitly assented to. We've seen that craving can quickly mushroom into grasping, particularly when it resonates with our deeply ingrained karmic formations. It proliferates quickly in dependence upon what we view to be our "needs."

That sense of "need" carries always a dualistic, survival impera-tive, even when the experienced need has nothing to do with physical safety. Regardless of what any compulsion is about, if our attention is lost in it, we hold it as absolutely necessary for survival. Unmindful, we fall into line and blindly follow the compulsion, and attention is hooked. The bait has been taken.

Grasping is a condition of almost irresistible desire, arising in a crescendo of compulsion. It can be overwhelming. Ask someone in recovery. When we're unmindful, these powerful recycling dynamics operate below awareness. Most of the moments in our lives that we have held with regret or remorse or guilt or shame arose when our attention was ensnared in grasping.

Just reflect on that for a moment, if you would. Our sense of identity is so confused that we add extra layers of guilt and shame to it as, with-out wisdom, we identify with actions that are not who we are but are, rather, conditioned and mindless reactive patterns. It is beneficial and necessary to examine our lives, to be sure. In that way, by recognizing our harmful actions we can strengthen our virtuous intention to live harmlessly. That is the power of sincere remorse. Guilt and shame are simply more habitual, harmful actions. When they arise, the response of wisdom to them is compassion.

THE CONDITION, BECOMING, refers to the moment identification utterly merges with wanting. We have seen how attention blindly follows grasping. Becoming is the identity of the blind follower of the grasping. Who we think we are grabs the opportunity to feed, to preserve the sense of its continued existence. Under the influence of ignorance, becoming functions with belief in the "I"-illusion and seeks, for that "I," a hoped-for release from the discomforting impulses of grasping. Becoming allows the "I"-illusion to seek to become the ensurer of what it believes to be its own better future.

The compulsion, personalized in becoming, is not just to satisfy the urge but to be the person, the entity, who goes about satisfying and, thus, will have the experience of being satisfied. It posits agency in a dualistic world and satiation in terms of self-reference. This is what is meant by *becoming*.

We all have myriad examples of this condition at play in our own minds. We live in a culture where consumerism is rampant. We buy the marketing. We contact, feel positive, crave, grasp, and wish to become the possessor of whatever it is that caught our attention. We contact, feel negative, crave, grasp, and wish to become the destroyer or avoider of whatever it is that caught our attention. Either way, we've become "someone."

Becoming is a proliferating force, magnifying both the force and speed of the spinning cycle, and rushing us to a nametag. If there's wanting, there must be an "I" wanting. If there's a verb, ignorance whispers, there must be a noun. The condition, *becoming*, is prepared to usher in the birth of a "someone," to impel attention toward the noun, "I."

In Sanskrit the term for this link is *bhāva*. Bhāva is thirst. The thirst is to take on identity and to satisfy the compulsive grasping with which the egoic self identifies. It deepens our habit patterns and seemingly validates—it certainly more deeply ingrains—the separate self-sense. In the hope for future contentment, it reinforces all past tendencies that have always led to suffering, keeping the miserable wheel going. We all have heard the definition of insanity as the hope that doing the same thing over and over again will lead to different results. Most of us just haven't taken it to heart. Like a baby as it's rocked in a carriage, we're lulled back to sleep in the repetitive circling of the conditions of unexamined mind.

We could say that the egoic sense of self, the "I"-illusion, is someone we're not. The dynamics we're exploring reveal how we become someone we're not, how attention becomes trapped in illusion. We become someone we're not with astonishing frequency, as all of us who are longing to awaken are only too well aware. Under the spell of becoming, we posture even to ourselves and become increasingly lost and confused—bound—in the process.

It is no wonder "imposter syndrome"—that pervasive sense we are somehow duping others into accepting us—is endemic. Each of us has our own version of it. We base our own version on a conceptually assumed personal inadequacy. At the level of the heart, wisdom recognizes that ego—inadequate in its incomplete accounting of who we are, impoverished and deluded in its sense of separation, and tenuous in its flimsy basis—is, in itself the inadequacy. Ego is the imposter. With practices such as these we're engaging in, it is possible to crown our essential nature in ego's place and repurpose ego's functionalities in service to the crown.

Becoming someone we're not operates on a spectrum of levels, from gross to subtle. Becoming is entangled with and conditioned by desire. It is confused by ignorance. We can witness it in some of our "superstitious" behavior. Is there a ritualistic way we have sex or we hold a golf club or relate to colleagues, hoping that what led to a few satisfying outcomes in the past might lead to one again? Where are we on the continuum of the need to control? What do we hope to gain or to avoid with that control?

Have we, for example, tried to emulate the thoughts and practices and postures—both physical and mental—of a past meditative "high" in the hopes of regaining it? All we're saying with that willful effort is that, at the moment, we don't like what is happening in our meditation now. We're saying we know better than grace, that grace doesn't seem to be doing a very good job.

Our attempts to choreograph a meditative experience are the strategies of self. For as long as we remain "the strategizing self" meditating, our attention will be utterly bound in ignorance—not free, not available to enter boundless freedom.

Pause for a bit, if you like, and take some time to quiet the mind. Call to recollection the "game faces," costumes, and masks you put on and the ploys, techniques, and strategies you employ. We posture when we do not recognize our holy and essential nature. Notice that each such posture and mask adds to the already heavy burden of "self." With each one, ask the question, what does this posturing hope to gain?

Ask, how identified am I with each mask or posture? Who would I be without it? Who do I imagine I am? Just inquire. See if you can witness the condition of *becoming*, wishing an identity to continue into the future; see if you can feel it as a proliferating force.

Becoming has a future orientation. There's a cartoon, one friend speaking to another, saying, "I want to learn to live in the moment— just not this moment." Becoming seeks future existence. Sometimes it seeks future nonexistence as a hoped-for avoidance of the experience of suffering. This is "suicidal panic," the "out" we seek when feeling utterly cornered in overwhelming psychic pain.

Becoming seeks the next condition, *birth*. Becoming keeps us ever hoping, ever enticed by the illusory rewards churned out by the system of suffering. Talk about false advertising! Talk about bait and switch! There is nothing in the cycling conditions that will bring us to the happiness we seek, nothing that will lead us any more fully to union with ever-present grace.

The condition of becoming is not to be confused with Being. Becoming is a dynamic factor in a system of illusion and the suffering an illusion-based life leads to. Being is an illusion-free state, a truth and the reality of our essential nature. Just as self is not present in love or in pure, deep gratitude, the tensed conditions of becoming and birth are not present in the surrendered ease of Being.

Becoming arises as an expression of incompleteness. Being is whole—lacking nothing, needing nothing. Becoming blocks the recognition and experience of being. Each time attention zooms through this condition in the cycle, we trade a mask for the truth.

Sit for a bit more, if you wish, in a mind even more quieted, even more able to see clearly. Looking even more deeply, we can ask, can I remain here, nameless, in this silent moment? What pulls me away?

And, each time we notice the tug out of here, out of now, the tug back into self, simply surrender the impulse and the pattern of becoming, surrender the wish for any identity other than our own true nature, the awareness in which we rest.

Rest. Rest without the need to become. Rest in Being.

BUDDHA POINTS OUT that "this holy life is lived for the abandonment of becoming." The abandonment of becoming is often called "the lion's roar," the expression of utter freedom and utter majesty. It is so, as mystic poet David Whyte observes that "inside everyone is a great shout of joy waiting to be born."

BECOMING

May we recognize the condition of becoming every time it arises—noticing its need to be "the one who," its need for the nametag, recognizing it as merely egoic hope for future contentment. Having seen where the nametag leads us—to a new "self," a new birth, new suffering—surrender becomes a joy. Simply being, with no need for becoming, becomes an ease and a refuge.

22

Birth

THE ENTIRE SYSTEM of dependent arising is driven in such a way as to confirm the existence of self. It processes sense data and interprets meaning in a way that supports our believed sense that we are who we think we are and that the world is as separate from us as it appears. The entire system filters information into and through a tightly bound paradigm. That paradigm is, nevertheless, a sleight of hand, a web of illusion unrecognized as illusion within ignorance.

We have seen, in contemplation, with deep reflection that the sense of self is—and knows itself to be—foundationally tenuous. Ignorance keeps us backing away, turning away, from that truth. It lures us away with the hope of fulfilling self's hunger for continued existence—our false refuge. Confrontation with the illusory nature of our self-sense and our self-beliefs appears as deeply threatening, possibly life ending. We so want to keep ourselves "formed." When ego is all we know, we allow attention to stay in the orbit of words, beliefs, and suffering.

Craving is powerful. The ever-present seed of egoic self germinates and takes root with craving. The seed of egoic self clings to craving for confirmation. "I want, therefore I am." Grasping and becoming seemingly provide the relief of the craving with which the sense of self identifies. Unmindful, we assent to such flimsy "evidence," such spurious proofs of existence. A. H. Almaas calls ignorance "a laziness in the soul regarding truth and reality."

We are fortunate to have the legacies of awakened beings. They point us toward wise view, where we can recognize for ourselves the mistaken and illusory nature of the beliefs that bind us. Through our practice, we've proven over and over that seeing is liberation. It leads us to recognize grace as our own essential nature.

Buddha insisted all that he had to offer would remain mere words—words with great potential to devolve into dogma—if we do not look for ourselves and recognize the truth in our own mind. The necessity for each of us to follow our own unique path of contemplation and growing illumination is echoed in Western tradition as well. Ephesians 5:14 suggests a path of seeing as it proclaims, "Anything exposed to light turns into light itself."

We have been bringing shadowed illusions into the light throughout our inquiry.

On this binding, spinning wheel, the force *to become* moves quickly and decisively into birth. New moment, new world, new "self." Same "I" label.

We cling—a precarious clinging when we view it with some mindful attention—to the notion *that* we are. Trapped attention does not have the capacity to notice that the "who" we believe ourselves to be is ever changing, just as the eddy cannot recognize that it is always formed from new water. The condition, *consciousness*, operates to obscure the condition, *birth*—the transition to a new self. "Self" is born into a new moment again and again, a transition that takes place swiftly.

The vastness of our essential nature becomes profoundly, sorrowfully limited with the "I" label. Nevertheless, unmindful, we attempt to hold and fixate, to diminish, the wondrous unfolding of grace with all our labels—especially "I" and "me" and "mine."

Consciousness obscures the rapid re-placement of the nametag, "I," on a new *someone*. It functions to occlude the gaps in the transition, thereby obscuring the grace that is always shining through. Those gaps are like the revelation of light when the clouds clear. Ignorance prefers clouds and shadow, the blind eye.

The condition, *ignorance*, holds the label, "I," applied by name-and-form as denoting something more than the simple convenience of label. It applies label heavy-handedly. Within the cycle of suffering, the "I" label is pinned to a series of illusions other than—and so much less than—the essential nature of our individual manifestation.

Each birth deepens the imprint for more unconscious "birth" to function without impediment. These limited someones arise within different time frames simultaneously. Birth manifests in the time frame of a book, a chapter, a paragraph, a sentence, sometimes even of a word in the course of our lives. Let's look at birth's function and force within the different time frames so that we come to recognize it.

The condition, *birth*, manifests most obviously in our birth into a precious human life. In this time frame, the time frame of a book, birth initiates us into a lifespan. Even at birth, our experience of being is conditioned by karmic formations—think gender, race, our genetic legacy—and all the other stage-setting links.

"I" is birthed first into a body sense—an unconscious and undifferentiated "I"-sense experienced bodily. Over time and with movement through the karmic formation of human developmental stages, we arise in the birth of the emotional "I." With this birth, we arise as a separate self. With emotion, we posit "other" based on emotional needs sensed and the wish for their fulfillment. This emotional "I" transcends the sense of "I" as only body while still retaining our tendency to regard body—its vulnerable flesh and breath—as "me."

With further development, we arrive with a sense of "I" that is largely mental. The *mental ego* is our belief in the illusion created by all the conditioning factors. The mental ego transcends a sense of self as purely emotional while retaining our tendency to identify with our emotions and physicality. These are births of "I" as chapters.

Such births—slightly less obvious than our physical birth but easily discernible within any pause to discern—continue throughout our lives in the form of the transitions that mark our meaningful life passages. We can think of our own lives and reflect on how the longer chapters were sustained by repeated turns of the wheel in shorter sequences. We often let the same story with the same storyteller echo and re-echo for a long time, deepening our conviction in the truth of it with each reverberation.

We want to recognize the condition, *birth*, in its propensity to rapidly arise as well, in the time frame of a sentence or a word. We want to be able to catch birth at work in our own minds.

With our pauses and inquiries, we may have begun to recognize the connection of the egoic self-sense with wanting. We can witness, with more clarity and mindful attention, the rapidity of identification with the felt need for the satisfaction of a compulsion—the almost instantaneous pairing of an "I" with a "want."

The birth of a new "I" can, and often does, happen in a moment. This is the *bok chuk* speed of the cycle, at the rate of a thought's sentence or even word. This is the birth of the "I" who scratched the itch, who hit the one-click option on Amazon, who vented the outrage. The sense of "I" birthed by the entire system of suffering leads to a someone—an illusory, temporary pull back from the abyss of not being someone. Over and over, we trade the seeming comfort of illusion for the truth.

The longer we practice and inquire, the more we discover that the comfort is also an illusion. As we've already discussed, most of what we call comfort is actually "changing suffering"—the ending of one suffering in exchange for the beginning of another. There's always another itch, another "must-have" item only a click away, another compelling bit of outrage to indulge in.

We thirst for the new and better *someone*, the safer and happier *someone*, the more perfect or more comfortable or "enlightened" *someone*. And the wheel keeps turning with the force of this misguided desire, keeps carving out deeper and deeper ruts for its own continued cycling.

If we look closely with ingathered attention at the rapid iteration of the "I"-illusion, we see the spinning impermanence. Typically, we only recognize the truth of impermanence in its most flagrant testimonials—a death, a divorce, a broken wineglass. We will explore this when we look at the last link, aging-and-death.

Take some time, if you would, and inquire. Look to see the someone you believe yourself to be in this moment. This is a "self" seed, a karmic formation, yearning for fruition, yearning to sustain itself through familiar action and reaction. We continually birth our narrative, our proclamation that "I am this."

To really see our psychic orientation to "re-incarnation," we can examine how we want others to see us. We can ask, who is the someone I want them to see? Who is the someone I'd rather they didn't see? And—even closer to the bone—who is the someone I want to think of as myself?

Note the experience of attention bound to this someone. Is it tight? Confused? Proud? Ashamed? Despairing? Angry or denying? We can recognize those qualities as the calling cards of ignorance and ignorance's colleagues.

Just look. And recognize. We're looking at the confusion of ignorance. Try stepping back and expanding to a more panoramic view. Isn't there a bit more clarity, a sense of being unbound within the awareness that is aware of those samsaric thoughts?

Rest there for a bit. Awareness's light is always that of wisdom and of a spacious freedom. With wisdom, we always choose awakening over sleepwalking. With wisdom, we choicelessly choose our essential nature over a contracted illusion with suffering always following in its wake.

We can catch the condition of *birth* at work in a bit less rapid but still ever-changing time frame—the speed of paragraphs within a chapter—by looking at the various functions we appear to fill each day and week and year. We inquire into the birth of new identities with the various functions such as parent, child, partnered person, single one. And we might inquire further: Am I like Atlas with the weight of the world on my shoulders, Narcissus gazing in the pool, or Sisyphus with the damn boulder? Am I the caregiver or the waited upon? The one who robotically apologizes or the one who never apologizes?

What hats do I identify with this very day, this week, this year? How does each hat sustain the "I"-thought? How does each hat mistake *process* for a single, continuing separate entity, "me"?

Pause and take some time for this inquiry, if you would. Identify the hats. In your imagination, try taking off each hat—slowly, one by one. Feel the increasing sense of lightness. And rest in what remains.

Refresh your being in what remains.

WE CAN RECOGNIZE the condition of birth with the acquisition of new functions, and we will note the condition, *aging-and-death*, with the relinquishment of functions we've come to take for granted. We can see that, since the system is ever responding to mutually influential conditions—in an ever-oscillating, ever-vibrating web—different births happen over different periods of time.

Birth places us in time and subject to the rules of time. Every birth leads to a death. We die because we're born. We've shed a thousand former selves along the way from the first date to the second date that will be in our obituary.

There have been many, many moments of birth in each of our lives to date. Who have you believed yourself to be? What do these senses of self and the belief in them have to do with our essential nature? What direction do they point attention toward? Can we see how the system is complicit in keeping us bound?

Again, no judgment needed. Simply note. Every pause we've taken to see leads to our unbinding. We can trust that. We can trust that it is grace calling us to see, and we can trust that grace longs for us as much as we long for grace. We can take heart.

Seeing the illusory nature of the separate self-sense, we increasingly rest in our essential nature. We begin to recognize, with dignity and with humility, that the work of grace within us is not only for ourselves. It is for all of manifestation, for the endless ever-unfolding, ever-evolving plenitude of interbeing. In Christian terminology, it is a brightening of our individual light in the Body of Christ.

The world—referred to in some traditions as "the sorrowful planet"—is convulsing in suffering at the moment. Perhaps it always has been. We have such privilege, such opportunity, the blessings of so many teachings. It becomes our responsibility, in the face of such suffering and in gratitude to such privilege, to cooperate with grace, to surrender to it, to allow it to transform, awaken, and unbind us. It's our privilege and it's our responsibility to be peace, to be sanity, to be justice and kindness, to be grace, to be both living witness and offering.

May *that* be the first conscious birth we take.

23

Aging-and-Death
(Suffering)

EVERY TURN OF THE WHEEL of the conditions of dependent arising—whether it be a lifetime or a chapter or even a brief momentary appearance of the "someone" with whom attention identified—ends in aging and death. It ends in suffering.

"Where there is this, there is that," Buddha said. Where there is self, there is suffering.

Although suffering has been inherent in the web of twelve mutually vibrating conditions all along, aging-and-death functions as the great "reveal" of the first noble truth. Aging-and-death underscores the pain inherent in self-reference. The clueless, confused round of existence that we call the everyday life of everyday self is an experience of contraction—often troubled, often difficult, often lonely.

Every sequence of becoming, of identifying with an "I"-illusion, ends in suffering. We are the fools who rush in. In a flashing moment's sequence, the spin ends in an aging and death that's barely noticed. Think of the "self" who is praised by his or her boss at the end of a day, for example, and walks out to the parking lot to find his or her car has been burglarized. The death of the first "self" is barely noticed as the second "self" is so rapidly born.

For a turning of the wheel that lasts a chapter in our lives, the spin ends in the aging and death of an identity as well as its attachments, assumptions, agreements, and appearances. It ends in a "little death." Think of the moment when you recognized the end of your youth. With my youngest daughter, I recognized a single moment as the last time I would push her in a swing. I was with another of my daughters the first time she was called "ma'am." She was shocked. One of her chapters ended.

We have such chapters in our spiritual growth as well. We don't, ordinarily, zoom into "enlightenment"—into an awakened relationship with life—in one fell swoop. Awakening is usually a gradual process marked by stages—chapters. We evolve through levels of awareness characterized by increased inclusivity, expanded identity, clearer knowing, and the increasing emergence of the noble qualities, the gifts of spirit.

Each of these stages becomes home base for a while, the locus of attention identifying as an "I." The "I" in each succeeding developmental stage is wispier. Each "I," though, comes to its own time of aging and death, preceded by the chaotic resistance and discomfort that accompany any death. We will speak of this process of transformation—from chaos to surrender to transcendence—in part five of *Unbinding*.

For the turning of the wheel that lasts a lifetime, the sequence ends in the illness, aging, and death of the physical body of our individual manifestation. With our own physical aging and death, we will no longer be able to deny the truth of suffering. From the perspective of ego—the mind that knows itself only as small and separate—the anguish as the end of life comes near is stark and terrifying.

Although suffering is always present behind the scenes—the ghost at the feast—the system as a whole functions to obscure this first noble truth. Ignorance brushes the truth of suffering away. It sweeps up the litter of suffering's thousand clues. Ignorance blames its own mental images of "others," of situations, and of personal "inadequacies" for the litter. It ignores the truth of suffering and averts our eye.

Consciousness keeps us rushing forward over the reality of our situation, rushing much too quickly to process any glimpse of truth. In willful denial of consequences, craving for becoming wants nothing in its way. Craving that has mushroomed into grasping will, like a bully, silence any objections and muscle out any obstacles. We've all watched ourselves do this at times—times when we've even violated our own moral compasses following the desire to have things be the way we want them to be. Becoming, clinging to an "I" paired with "want," leads to birth. And birth meets its match in inevitable aging and death, confronting a far greater power—the truth of life-in-form.

Suffering is in every strand of the complex web of the conditions of dependent arising. The web is a dust collector, collecting malaise and sorrows within its confines. Suffering is the inevitable result of the interplay of factors. With suffering—arising so undeniably in aging and death—we recognize the consequence of all the "becoming" we so hopefully agreed to. Buddha reminds us starkly: "The end of collection is dispersion. The end of rising is falling. The end of meeting is parting. The end of birth is death."

Although hope springs eternal in the desires of self, the system of samsara is a closed and tangled system. It does not lead to fulfillment.

It requires endless unrequited hope and desire to keep it spinning. Without inquiry, the system maintains its function. With unfailing consistency, it produces self and suffering. Suffering will remain until we explore and clearly see through the factors churning out the "I"-illusion with the sane mind of wisdom. Blessed be the explorer.

THERE ARE PREDICTABLE SUFFERINGS in a human life. Impermanence is the mark of all existence. Every last one of our deepest attachments—our attachments to our close circle of loved ones—will end in parting. A thought in an old Sanskrit verse has always struck me about our relationships: "Two bits of driftwood might meet on the great ocean. Having touched they shall drift apart. The encounters of all creatures are like this." It's a vivid visual, reminding us of how fleeting and precious is this life and all beings in it. It's a reminder that gratitude and awe are among our most appropriate responses to the privilege of sharing even a moment of life with beloveds.

Aging, illness, and death are inevitable. One way or another, we will be separated from those we love. One way or another, we will be pulled away from our possessions, our accomplishments, our identities. These predictable sufferings will inevitably bring attention to illusion's dead end. We will no longer be able to pretend we are unaware of suffering. We will come face to face with it. We will recognize the absurdity of hoping we can outwit life, that we can make life be the way we want it to be. The illusory bubble will burst, and only truth will remain.

Aging, illness, and death are our predictable sufferings. There is nothing we can do to change this truth, to change reality. We are already on death's trajectory. Not a single one of us—awake or asleep—is an exception. Buddha died from sickness, encouraging awakening and leaving behind wisdom. Jesus died on the cross, making an offering of his suffering and leaving behind love. The predictable sufferings come to us all.

It seems to me that confronting our mortality, surrendering to the truth of impermanence, is one of the three great tasks of awakening—along with stilling the mind and opening the heart. Each of us has the capacity to fulfill the great tasks, and each of us has grace's cooperation in so doing.

Thai Buddhist teacher Ajaan Lee called aging, illness, and death our three greatest teachers. He called them, "Noble teachers, noble jewels. If they were people, I would bow down to their feet every day." "Heavenly messengers," each offers us a profound spiritual opportunity. It is possible to work with this condition, *suffering*, consciously.

In the process of dying, a spiritual transformation of immeasurable proportions takes place. As we die, the conditions of obscuration and denial will no longer hold sway. Ego's props—the psychological and physical conditions that have sustained and upheld the separate sense of self—are stripped away. As they dissipate, attention trapped in the "I"-illusion they created is released. At physical death, there is an exquisite calibration that leads attention directly into the grace that has always been present. As nondual teacher Jeff Foster puts it, "Your absence is the stunning presence of Life." The "I"-illusion evaporates, and all that remains is the grace that has always been right here, right now.

In the midst of life, we can allow this same transformation. Contemplation increasingly recognizes illusion as illusion. Egoic props are seen to be insubstantial. They are seen to be fabrications which no longer have the power to enchant us. Surrender becomes easier and more spontaneous. Releasing the props, the "I"-illusion which had been sustained by them simply dissolves. There is no longer an obstruction to grace; the imagined separation from the sacred no longer exists. This is the work we have been doing throughout our discussion. We will look at this even more closely in the next section.

WE HAVE LOOKED at the first noble truth throughout our discussions. Looking again can deepen our realization of it. Our experiential realization is dependent upon the depth of the clear seeing that grace grants us in accordance with our intention. In equal measure, our realization will be as transformative as our depth of penetration into the illusions created by the whole cycle.

It is not easy to be a person. We know that in our own experience.

We hold our children close when they are little—how we wish we could spare them the sorrows of humanity! Imagine if we widened our circle of caring to include every being, every manifestation of grace. Our heart would beautifully break open, and self would disappear in the purifying power of compassion. Suffering can serve our awakening.

Our "less intense" instances of suffering are a fertile field in which to begin a deliberate investigation. Recollecting such moments, recognizing suffering, we can work with a measure of wisdom and skill. Disappointment, quiet despair, malaise, and difficulty make their appearance in every human life. We all have our own litanies spanning a continuum of possibilities for suffering—from financial worries to crushing loss.

Right now, it can be useful to bring to mind instances of some of our "little deaths." We've looked at suffering before from a slightly different perspective. We inquired into the tight and binding grip of self. We've recognized how it feels to be trapped in self. We've come to see the suffering in self.

Looking now, we're inquiring from a slightly different angle. We're looking to see self in suffering. We're looking at how, by taking impersonal circumstances personally, we increase their painful impact.

Universal human reactions such as grief, shock, trauma, and moral injury demand our compassion. Those commonalities of our humanity—the predictable sufferings of aging, illness, and death that will visit us all—are not what we're looking at here. Right now, we're looking specifically at the way we've personalized suffering. We color suffering with self-reference and thereby double the weight of it. We do it with the "Why me?" thoughts, suggestive of the willingness to allow "someone else" to endure it. We do it with self-pity, with the imploding despair of what a challenging circumstance means to "me."

It would be helpful to pause for a moment and note the suffering we've endured as we've clung to who we believe ourselves to be. This demands a bit of equanimity, a quieted mind still enough to recollect and witness without falling into victimhood, anger, or self-pity. It demands, as does every other moment in our life, that we rest in essence—the "soul" at the midpoint between our humanity and our divinity.

So, if you will, pause and allow the mind to quiet. Allow the mind to balance in equanimity. Use the pause as a structured reflection. Recall some of the "little deaths," the moments of suffering you have experienced. And, from that balance point, simply see. Honestly see. Open to what's revealed in the inquiry.

Whatever are the unique recollections that arise for you, notice how "I" was so present. Note how the nakedly revealed ego scrambles in the inquiry when its known world suddenly shifts. Notice the self-referential reactivity involved in the circumstances we hold as suffering. Note the swirling upset within the thoughts about how the circumstances impacted you. Note what you thought the circumstances meant about you, how they injured or affronted the self-sense, how they threatened the self's desire for comfort.

Self and suffering always co-arise. Suffering is the cost of self-ing. It is the price exacted when we identify with and cling to the "I"-illusion that arises in the interaction of the twelve conditions of samsara.

Just open to seeing. Rest in the openness that sees for a while. Rest in the contemplative poet Stephen Levine's quiet realization: "No one in the boat; no one to suffer." Let your heart soften in compassion for all that has been endured in bondage to self. Let it break wide open.

THE REALIZATION of the truth of suffering is a momentous, fundamentally transformative turning point. In recovery programs, this honesty is the first step in living life with a new direction. Seeing, we can clearly acknowledge that we have been powerless over our addiction—whether that be to substances or to ego—and that our lives have become unmanageable within the addiction. There is an undefendedness in such clear acknowledgment, a budding sense of truth as refuge.

The moment we proclaim, "Enough!" is the moment of the great turn, the great reversal in our desiring and in our hunger. The eddy begins to get a glimmer of recognition that, in essence, it is not other than the stream.

In Buddhism, four contemplations are suggested to assist us in this great reversal, this great renunciation of samsaric attachment. The four contemplations, often called the four "reminders"—like grace whispering in our ear—are reflections on the preciousness of this human life, the necessity of confronting our mortality, the recognition that thoughts and actions condition consequences, and the realization of the suffering inherent in unconscious existence. It is wise to reflect deeply and often upon each of these reminders.

The last link in the cycle of dependent arising, aging-and-death, reveals itself—without question—as suffering. Without a deep and profound recognition of the absurdity of continuing to allow attention to remain bound in the cycle, ignorance will continue with the spinning proliferation of self and suffering. Suffering offers itself, again and again, to our recognition, our acknowledgment.

To recognize suffering as suffering—to call it by name and to discern its origins—is wisdom. Here is our opportunity to release attention from its binding. Over and over, we have the opportunity to recognize the grace that is allowing us to view our predicament with wisdom. Over and over, we have the opportunity to trust that the compassion of grace will lead us home to where we have ever been—our own essential nature, that balance point of our Buddha nature and our human nature.

There is a beautiful story of an awakened Buddhist teacher, Marpa. Surrounded by his students, he heard the news of his son's death and began to weep. His students were confused and said to him, "But you have taught us to dwell in the birthless, deathless state. Why are you weeping?" Marpa answered simply: "Because this death is the death of my son."

We don't awaken *from* our humanity, we awaken *into* it.

IN THE NEXT SECTION, we will explore further skillful ways to free ourselves from the whole system of self and suffering. The wisdom of seeing, as we have begun to recognize, weakens the system's hold on our attention, ultimately collapsing the system entirely.

The Buddhist mystic Alan Watts realized that "what you are basically, deep, deep down, far, far in, is simply the fabric and structure of existence itself." That fabric and structure is one of relationality, of conditionality. To awaken we work with conditionality consciously.

We turn now to explore how to work with the very system that creates self and suffering skillfully and mindfully, in service to awakening.

PART FIVE

Surrender

24

Seeing

THROUGHOUT OUR EXPLORATION and contemplation, we've kept returning to a single significant focus, a pivotal point. In any number of ways, we've inquired into the first noble truth, the truth of suffering.

When death comes to call we will be unable to deny that truth. In this inquiry we've engaged in together my hope is that each of us has come to a deeper, clearer recognition that not only is suffering present at the end of life, but there is endemic suffering—great and small—in a life bound within illusion.

Every becoming is stressful, and every becoming ends. Every time a turn of the wheel of dependent arising knocks us around in robotic, uncomfortable, defended habits and deposits us at aging-and-death, we have an opportunity for this realization. How many times have we been around this block mindlessly, only to sign on for another lap? To know samsara for what it is allows us to know ourselves for what we are.

We have already—as practitioners, as mystics—awakened our only beneficial desire: our hunger for the sacred, the desire to release and surrender trapped attention into awareness beyond self. We all have a natural tropism toward the sacred, like a sapling seeking the sun. Our yearning for the sacred comes to us from grace. This arises initially in us as longing, and then as intention. Intention creates a shift in our experience of being, an interest in and a willingness to practice contemplation and self-surrender out of a growing wish to draw close to and live within sacred presence.

Without mindful attention, we have lived in the illusion of separation, lost and alone in the confusion of mindless internal dialogue. Each of us, in our own way and in our honest self-reflection, has acknowledged the chronic malaise of a life lived in limitation, at a remove from truth. And each of us has come—through our inquiry—to acknowledge the truth of impermanence, the absence of any reliable refuge within the fleeting, impersonal conditions of samsara and the illusions they create. Such direct experiential realizations—arising from seeing—transfigure our being.

Buddha, as we have seen, defined wisdom as "the knowledge and vision of things as they really are." Our acknowledgment of suffering is a pivotal realization, as is the realization that any moment of genuine happiness we've ever had was a moment of self-forgetfulness. Our realizations wake us up to the truth and leave us hungering for more. They deepen our commitment to recognize, have confidence in, and begin to embody awareness far beyond only self, far beyond only form—utterly free of the illusory orbit of "separation."

Recognition is liberation. We have repeated that phrase often throughout our conversation. It is a beneficial mantra. It serves as our reminder to continue to look at what is actually so, to see through the conditioning processes that create the illusion of egoic self and the endlessly changing appearances of "other." We want to see through them just enough to unweave the fabrications that bind our attention within their entangling web. Atisha, the great eleventh-century

Buddhist mystic, counseled that "the greatest wisdom is seeing through appearances."

Seeing, we can liberate ourselves from the deep, inarticulate hope of the "I"-illusion, that eddy in the stream. We can begin to witness the thoughts that have always kept attention bound in believing and desiring. We are now familiar with the conditions of dependent arising and can begin to witness their interplay. We can begin to simply observe them appearing and dissolving, like falling snowflakes melting on our hand. We can begin to recognize, as Buddha recognized: "Thus come, thus gone."

Insight into what is so is a path of liberation. We can observe the entire system of self and suffering, within our own psychological and physical experience, within our own mindbody. Doing so, we come to learn the value of applying mindful attention in all of the moments of our life—exploring, inquiring, and asking the essential question: What's going on here?

Our willingness to inquire demands (and cultivates) a willingness to surrender our "known world" and explore beyond our unexamined "certainties." The poet David Whyte speaks of coming to a place whose "only task is to trouble you" with requests to stop what you are doing and who you are becoming—a place with questions that "lead everywhere, questions that can make or unmake a life."

The value of simply looking has been recognized in many wisdom lineages. Although often abused, misappropriated, and misunderstood throughout the centuries, the sacrament of confession holds liberative potential in its depths. Nondual Indian mystic Ramana Maharshi used questioning as his central practice, his path. Thomas Merton searched for his—our—"basic natural unity" through the questions he asked in the silence and solitude he recognized as essential for awakening.

Our practice of insight has a wide range—from glimpsing to profound and stable realization. It includes moments of seeing and understanding that can weaken the closed system of self and suffering by degrees. The system weakens in those glimpses of insight simply because—through seeing—we become less inclined to eagerly fuel it, to feed it with our attention.

The range of seeing's power extends to insights so intense that, like shock waves, they can shatter our own uniquely personal paradigm of samsara along with all the conditions that sustain it. Insight has the potential to destroy the structural stability of the system of dependent arising, leaving it without the power or means to any longer capture our attention.

Wisdom, at its full depth and power, utterly uproots ignorance. Without ignorance functioning, the system no longer traps and binds. We can bring discerning wisdom to any and every one of the conditions of dependent arising. Each is under the sway of ignorance. That shadowed sway is extinguished in the light of wisdom.

We simply need to keep looking. It's a bit of a chore to keep reminding ourselves to look at first, to be sure. But mindful attention evolves into the enlivening state of wonder and on into ever-deepening awe as we are increasingly able to bear the radiance and power of grace.

Having acknowledged the first noble truth, we have seen that curiosity arises about the second noble truth—the truth of the origin of suffering. It's like waking up and finding yourself alone and tied up in ropes. We look at the way the ropes are tied so that we might untie them.

We've spent time looking at and learning to recognize each of the twelve conditions of dependent arising. They've given us a template and a lexicon to identify and understand what we're looking at.

Through our pausing and contemplation, we know a bit about the ground environment of ignorance and karmic formations that allow and shape our habitual patterns of body, speech, and mind. We know a bit about the illusion-creating propensities of consciousness and name-and-form. Nothing has ever been what we believed it to be. We have only ever interacted with our own ignorance, our own fabricated mental images.

The stance of seeing, the willingness to pause and see, creates a tiny bit of distance—a wedge of dis-identification—between our attention and our images. The moment we see we are already "backed out of" that which binds. This is so with each and every mindful recognition of one of the twelve conditions.

Buddha advised us all to let go of that which we are not. We're beginning to see that we are not our habitual patterns and—in each moment of that recognition—have already released some attention from them. We've learned to keep things simple—to simply recognize confusion, complexity, and reactivity as signs of ignorance.

Recognition is enabled by grace. Thirteenth-century mystic St. Bonaventure reminded us all that "if you desire to know, ask for grace." Recognition comes from a view more expansive and clear-seeing than ignorance. It is the view from wisdom. The recognition of the presence of craving instantly allows curiosity about what's actually going on and, in that curiosity, we have already entered a wiser view. We step back into the equanimity of grace's awareness, ever present. The slightest shift in the locus of attention and identity creates a qualitatively transformed experience of being. Trapped attention returns to its home in formless awareness. Identification that had been bound in illusion is released into truth.

We've grown in our understanding of our mind's co-creation of appearances. However penetrating has been our understanding, to that degree we've relaxed our tight assumptions about the way things exist. We're no longer so likely, when mindful, to view the objects of appearance as existing in the way that they appear. We're no longer so likely to view them as separate, as "other," as inherently existing from their own side. We hold name-and-form, the capacity to label, much more lightly. We begin to recognize label as mere convenience in our conventional life. Ordinary appearances remain, but ordinary conceptions shift.

The relaxing of our tightly grasped "separation" has led, hopefully, to an increased sense of the dance of interbeing, of our communion in all of creation, manifest and unmanifest. This is the truth of *anattā*, the lack of separate, inherent existence of all phenomena including the self. A co-arising set of conditions produces the unending, wondrous display of grace. The relationship, the interbeing, is grace.

Pierre Teilhard de Chardin, the great Catholic mystic, noted, "We are one, after all, you and I. Together we suffer; together exist, and forever will recreate each other." Each of us would not be who we are in this moment without each other. We are all communicants in grace, ever evolving in infinite potentiality. It could not be otherwise.

Our realizations, at whatever degree of depth they have penetrated our being, have been many. Looking, we've seen the suffering inherent in the egoic self-sense; we've clearly seen the causes and conditions that produce the illusion of that self-sense—even as they arise in each moment. Looking, we've seen the powerful potential of the system of self and suffering to bind attention within it. With each degree of clear seeing's penetration of the illusions of ordinary mind, we are that much more free, that much more unbound.

Together, we've come to see the egoic sense of self as an overtone, a product, of all these ongoing processes, recognizing that who we believe ourselves to be is a mental fabrication—the buzzing noise of inner dialogue, an illusion of the "life support" system of dependent arising. It is not real. To identify as *someone* is no proof of the ultimate reality of that someone. To identify as someone is simply the dynamics of craving, grasping, and becoming at work under the cover of ignorance.

WHEN WE LOOK FOR "SELF," we see only its absence. We see the absence of what we expected to see. The egoic self-sense is not present as a condition of our being in life-in-form but as a harmonic of the ongoing unconscious processes we've been exploring.

Keep looking for it, if you like—especially when the sense of self is strong, as it is when conditioned by craving and grasping's reactivity. Except as mere thought and emotional familiarity, "I" and "me" will not be found. With continued investigation and inquiry, we are not quite as likely to believe in the reality of the sense of self for sustained periods as we have in the past.

We are not quite as likely or as willing to believe in the "I"-illusion— or find it attractive or constant or a comfort—especially after having focused deliberately on the suffering that is its inevitable companion. With continued practice and sustained intention, we develop the capacity to stare down the urge, the compulsion, for becoming, for being a "someone." We develop some capacity, as we increasingly rest in grace, to ride the waves of grasping. Having known spaciousness, we become disenchanted with limitation. We finally, thank goodness, grow in discernment.

We have begun to acknowledge the stress and effort of so much hiding and posturing, and have begun to see the egoic self-sense as illusion, as false refuge—utterly unreliable and an obstruction to all that lies beyond it. As we've recognized this, as we've seen more clearly—with a measure of joy, gratitude, and awe—we've found attention returning to its natural resting place in sacred awareness.

Natural great peace has equanimity. It is a refuge from compulsion. We're no longer so lured by the promises of gratification whispered—and sometimes shouted—by the unexamined dynamics of dependent arising. We find a new disenchantment with the endless display of seductive illusions. As we have with small talk and malls, worry and vanity, we begin to turn away. We become done, uninterested. Those seeds of potentiality are "cooked" and unlikely to germinate again. We begin the turn toward truth and what really matters. Illusion loses its allure when seen through.

Nibbida is a Pali word. It literally means "finding out." Finding out is what happens when we dare to look, and when we quiet enough to see. Finding out is what happens when we step out of ignorance and into wisdom. Remember that incredibly helpful question we can ask ourselves in any moment: What's looking now—ignorance or wisdom, self or grace?

Insight is a vehicle for our journey—the fourth noble truth. The path carries us from sleepwalking to awakening—the third noble truth. It is a joy and an affirmation to note our own movement into dignity and nobility—the blessing of the grace we are.

We have become, through our dedication and devotion, familiar with the grace from which we are inseparable. Surrender, a consideration which had been held by ego to be either weak or terrifying, becomes more willing, more joyful, when we understand that all we are surrendering is an illusion and the pain that accompanies it. A steadfast practice of self-surrender brings us to the recognition that there was never an "I" to surrender anyway. At that point, we just smile—just like Buddha.

LIBERATING VIEWS function to serve awakening. In the ignorance of ordinary mind, we still imagine we can unbind from suffering without unbinding from self. Our ordinary tendency may be to wish to find a strategy to unbind from the conditions of dependent arising. We may very well concoct various ways to outfox the system and attempt to deny or suppress its pull. We may try every adaptive tool we have in our spiritual-bypassing grab bags.

As we grow in wisdom and begin to mature spiritually, we begin to recognize that self and suffering cannot be separated. We, thankfully, begin to recognize that strategies are willful, egoic effort. They only strengthen the illusion of a self that arises within that system of suffering—a self that tries to tinker some accommodation with the system so that the egoic self-sense may continue.

Strategies are not transformative. Seeing is.

Rather than thinking in terms of strategies, we can think in terms of stance. Whereas a strategy keeps attention trapped in the "I"-illusion, a stance has to do with a conscious placement of our attention beyond self.

Our growing realization provides a new platform for our perspective, our view, our understanding, and our path.

Grace's platform is the truth—the recognition of what's so. The platform is courage—the willingness to look and remain looking rather than returning to believing. The platform is wisdom, the capacity to see clearly. The platform is surrender—the willingness to let go of the causes of suffering. Surrender is one of the sweetest practices of all. With surrender, as contemplative poet Jan Richardson notes, we turn our face "toward what had been always," our eyes "finally open in ancient recognition, willingly dazzled, illuminated at last."

25

The Sacrament of Surrender

TO OUR EGOIC SENSE OF SELF, even the idea of surrender looms as a terrifying fear of engulfment. Ego has a profound resistance to anything viewed as the certain disruption of imputed order, the certain death of what has been assumed, the certain end of becoming. We know that to be so.

Initially, on a spiritual path, we prefer comfort over the compromise we think we must make if we are to live our realizations. We can witness our reluctance—sometimes deep reluctance—to surrender what we still wish to hold on to.

We define ourselves by what we cling to. The reluctance to let go of the self-sense with which we've identified for so long can be felt as a scurrying in the mind. We can experience it. The wish to continue the samsaric cycle gathers its defensive justifications and rallies its hopeful desires. We can feel the protective conceptual rush respond to threatened, panicked self-cherishing.

As practitioners, we have a strong intuition that the separate sense of self will melt like a snowman in the sun when we let go of the definitions and the clinging, when we release the defendedness and the identification. That intuition can keep us paralyzed for a while. We can get a bit stuck between the habitual grasping at a self and the desire to awaken from that dream.

Most of us have some degree of attention still caught in samsara. We can find ourselves, at times, a bit conflicted and confused. Our longing for the sacred and our attachment to the "I"-illusion often play isometrics with each other, engaging for a long time in a well-matched tug of war.

It is not unusual to get caught for a while in an edgy, awkward spot, between the proverbial devil and the deep blue sea. We look behind us at the system of self and suffering and—by virtue of our growing realization—recognize that it holds nothing meaningful, essential, or true. We increasingly recognize that living in the illusion of separation is a waste of the gift of this precious human life, offered to us for awakening. We acknowledge the suffering inherent in samsaric existence. We're becoming disenchanted, more dispassionate.

We hear grace calling us. The heart resonates with a growing longing to follow, to take the leap of faith out beyond self. Looking back—we see the hopelessness of illusion. Looking forward—we pause in fear.

We recoil from the unknown and from a power we intuit as far greater than our flimsy but stubborn sense of self. Any one of us who holds the intention to awaken knows this fear. Richard Rohr points out that the single most repeated phrase in the Bible is "be not afraid."

We're stuck for a while at 50/50. Half of our attention is trapped in the familiar. Our habituated inclination is to tighten our fist around familiarity, grasping at remaining there. The other half of our attention is drawn by its own natural yearning for grace—like a child for its mother. Clear seeing brings attention to grace. Our desire to rest there increases. Our practice nurtures our intention to awaken and—with continued practice, we can count on it—the percentages shift from

50/50 to 49/51—the most significant one percentage point difference of our lives.

WE HAVE ENGAGED in inquiry throughout our discussion and have come to know for ourselves that the simple willingness to look, to defy the habit of ignorance, brings us face to face with truth no longer denied. To nurture a continuing transformative shift, we want to continue looking and seeing, practicing inquiry.

The capacity to surrender grows and deepens and becomes increasingly sincere the more we clearly know, at the level of the heart, the disadvantages of our old paradigm, the fabricated world of self and suffering. Chögyam Trungpa called ego "a succession of confusions." Surrender arises from the resolve of having clearly seen how far the succession of confusions has removed attention from the present, from the truth, and from communion in grace.

We surrender, increasingly and ever more whole-heartedly, when we see that the limitations of remaining bound within an "I"-illusion infinitely outweigh the benefits. We surrender when denial is no longer possible. Like a chick grown too big for the egg enclosing it, we peck our way out with each new insight, with each new act of surrender.

Surrender is a turn of attention out of ignorance and into the light of wisdom. The willingness to surrender, as we've seen and experienced in our own being, begins with the recognition of suffering as the predictable product of the whole cycle of samsara. Indeed, a deep realization of suffering leads naturally and spontaneously to surrender.

As practitioners, we don't remain paralyzed forever. At some point, having been stuck for a while on the precipice of surrender, we take the risk; or we are pushed or pulled into the risk (dying will certainly do that for us). We take the leap. We free fall into grace. St. John of the Cross followed the call in Luke 5:4 to "launch out into the deep." Buddha compared it to being released from slavery.

Most of us are led to surrender without choice for the first time— through the painful but transformative fields of disruption and chaos, through undeniable suffering. Every transformative shift that we experience—whether at the time of our death or a thousand times in the midst of a life of awakening—follows a simple sequence. It goes from chaos to surrender to transcendence.

The recognition of the system of dependent arising as a system of suffering is a universal recognition in all who see. To the degree we identify with the "I"-illusion, suffering initially elicits chaos.

Grace is the nature of everything, revealing itself often in beauty, in goodness, in wisdom. It also reveals itself in fierceness—all that Aeschylus called the "awful grace of God." In some ways, we could say that suffering—grace in its fiercest form—is a call to wake up, to look, to recognize our far remove from the refuge of the sacred, from all that is ultimately meaningful.

We have explored the notion that suffering is the experience of reality grating against ego. When the suffering—always endemic in the "I"-illusion—raises in volume and intensity, it crosses into the threshold of recognition. The experience of chaos is "self" recognizing suffering.

As much as we conspire to defend ourselves against it, suffering will make its presence known. When it does, attention locked within the world of appearances—locked in a form-only, self-only world— experiences chaos. Chaos, you could say, appears at the outward dimension of reality, just as roiling waves appear at the surface of the oceans' calm depths. Surface attention, the attention trapped in the web of self and suffering, experiences the turbulence and recoils. It strategizes, bargains, entreats, and denies—only to recognize that it has no power in the face of reality.

The recognition of chaos—as "self" recognizes suffering—begins as we start to open our eyes and awaken, whether that be in response to grace's call to enter a spiritual path, or whether that be through the experience of dying, the most profoundly transformative of spiritual paths. Prior to that, unmindfulness usually keeps us numb, entranced, sleepwalking.

The chaos that arises with attention's naked confrontation with the truth of suffering leads us to surrender. At some point, with every ploy exhausted, we recognize that there is no denial, no escape, no option other than surrender.

Buddha, in his commitment to awaken, vowed to remain under a tree until he became enlightened—fully awake. With the power of profound and focused attention, he witnessed the suffering and chaos of unexamined mind. His inquiry pierced deeply enough to see the dynamics creating it. Once seen, he abandoned all attachment to self and the factors of its creation. He utterly surrendered the passion for the cycle to continue. The passion dissipated in the seeing. In this transcendence of self and suffering, he became "one who has gone beyond." He offered the realizations of his wisdom so that they might become our own.

There is not a more beautiful example of surrender than the surrender of Jesus. He bore beautiful witness to awakening from the dream of self. In Gethsemane, Jesus was poignantly aware of his humanity—aware of self and doubt and clinging. Even with the depth of his realizations and the magnitude of his love, he experienced the angst of his own impending death.

He prayed—quieting his mind and opening his heart. Gethsemane was his passageway through the chaotic minds of clinging and fear, through the chaotic mind of passion. Letting go of any self-reference—releasing it into prayer and refuge in God's love—he surrendered. In love, for love, arms wide open on the cross, he emerged into Christ consciousness. Transcending the smallness of self, obliterating the separation self imposes, he revealed where absolute surrender leads. "Follow me," he said.

Surrender leads us home. Surrender leads directly to attention's transcendence of its limitation in ego. Attention, freed in transcendence, becomes available to abide as sacred pure awareness in immanence.

SURRENDER for Jesus and Buddha was utter and complete. They both pulled the "I"-illusion out by its roots. For most of us, surrender is more of a gradual process. We tend to be content with simply "weeding" for quite a while until—tired of the endless weeding—we finally yank the roots of "self" out of samsara's clutches.

Facing the facts, the truth of suffering and its causes, we become increasing willing—even eager—to simply surrender. We surrender the conviction that reality in this moment could be other than it is. We surrender the hopeful belief that samsara will someday deliver on its promises. We surrender the notion that any further tweaking of our "self" or of our circumstances will create a "better alternative" to reality.

Through the simple honesty of our sitting practice, we become increasingly willing to let go of what binds us—every ploy to blame, deny, define, suppress, modify, adapt, hope, fear, and rail against. We surrender every mistaken premise, one by one as they arise.

With continued surrender, we recognize that this action—arising from wisdom, arising from our longing for union, arising from grace— withers up the power of habitual patterns to control attention. The habitual patterns lose their appeal, their enchantment. With seeing and the surrender that follows naturally upon seeing, attention loses its susceptibility to seduction. We surrender our reliance on the distorted, misleading thoughts of conceptual mind.

Surrender lands us in increased freedom and in ripening capacity for love and compassion, for growing wisdom. As thread after thread of the binding web is relinquished—through understanding—there is a disengagement with the illusory phenomena of self and others and with every unexamined assumption. This is unbinding. With insight's power to clear away fabricated obstructions, we begin to follow— unimpeded and with increasing ease—the magnetic pull of grace.

SURRENDER SIGNALS the greatest transformative shift of a human life. Attention moves out of the shadows of ignorance and toward growing illumination. Surrender functions as an interruption, an abrupt application of the brakes, to the forward spinning momentum of the cycle of samsara, the cycle of endless rebirth, endless aging-and-death.

The apparent continuity of the "I"-illusion is halted during our moments of surrender. We give it up. Interrupting attention's identification with the patterned conditions of the spin, surrender allows a radical restructuring of our identity, our knowing, our capacity, and the nature of the offering of our individual manifestation.

With surrender, the momentum of beliefs is broken in awareness, ignorance is offset by wisdom, and attention is released into the boundless continuum of Being. We recognize not only the futility but the life-squandering of trying to find a more comfortable adjustment within samsara. With surrender, conventional dichotomies are transcended in an overhaul of our ingrained assumptions.

As we continue in our practice, we will come to recognize surrender as an "event horizon." Attention finds itself in a new home base within formless awareness. There is a radical transformation in the way continued experience is processed. Formless awareness—grace—allows us, through our practice, to see form as not what we believed it to be. When we see events purely as events, as processes in flux and transformation and not as entities, we can abandon our investment in them, our passion for them.

Surrender is not an adaptation, not an attempt to readjust within our familiar paradigm. It is not an egoic strategy but the spontaneous expression of heart-felt longing. It signifies a transformative shift and a deep and earnest wish to invite more transformative shifts, more deaths of old levels of functioning, more relinquishments of the desire to become a future new and improved "self." We no longer feed the beast. Buddha spoke not so much of attainment but of cessation.

In surrendering, all that is lost is the "idea" of "me." We simply engage in a practice of continuous willingness to surrender the thought, the illusion, upon recognizing its appearance.

On a committed spiritual path, a thought of "I" or "me" will sometimes arise with a cry and an urgency indicating a wound in need of healing before further awakening can proceed. In that case, we respond to it with gratitude that we have the opportunity to see and heal it. We respond with the courage of openness and with tender compassion. Otherwise, when one of the ten thousand daily thoughts of "I" arises, we recognize it has no value in service to awakening and we surrender it. As we've noted in our own experience, this becomes increasingly easy to do when we've seen not only its illusory nature but also the suffering inherent in the illusion.

Recognizing the difference between a shaky belief and the stability of a spiritual realization, we become increasingly willing to let go of the "merely believed" and increasingly willing to trust in grace's revelation and grace's lead. We release the "control" we previously imagined. We release the "I"-illusion we assumed *could* control, recognizing it as a source of suffering.

We continue to mindfully attend to what's going on in our habituated dynamics, to look and to see. It's not about attempting to change or deny what we see. Trying to eliminate the patterns is an egoic strategy. Any act of will, of volitional intent, springs from the condition, *karmic formation,* and keeps us distant from grace in a small, tight knot of self. To engage inquiry is to step back into a new stance of looking, one of wisdom.

Inquiry reveals. When we first begin a practice, "self" looms as solid, unassailable, unquestionable. We chip away at it, as if it were made of stone, with various practices—moral discipline, compassion cultivation, welcoming gestures, for example—designed to engage our more noble qualities.

With time and continued inquiry, our realization grows, illuminating the truth of "self" as illusory, as an interference pattern—nothing more. It is recognized as a crisscrossing weave of thought and habit and desire existing only in unexamined mind and obstructing our recognition of grace. What had seemed stone—the transformation of which would have required a Herculean effort of sculpting and chiseling—now is realized as only cobweb, easily undone by a baby's finger or a dying person's shallow breath.

As MYSTICS within any tradition, each of us has realized that grace moves in us as a stirring, a longing. It has been grace calling us all along to a radically new way to live—to an unbound life, a holy life, far beyond only self. Surrender is the willingness to let go of the habitual inclination to cede attention to anything other than grace.

The chaos that arises as "self" recognizes suffering leads us to surrender. And surrender leads directly to the transcendence of self's fixated view. Once freed from ignorance, attention moves into wisdom, into love. It moves into trust. We grow in our confidence. We begin to trust mindful attention for its power to unbind and recognize the capacity as a gift. We grow in our faith in grace and in the path grace provides and illuminates for each of us individually.

Buddha's wisdom puts this turnabout under a microscope. In the Upanisa Sutta, which encompasses the teachings on "transcendent" dependent arising, he observed that there is a near instantaneous arising of faith and confidence that accompanies penetrating realization of the truth of suffering, or the truth of the experience of the "I"-illusion. A. H. Almaas observed that "basic trust is the soul's way of attuning to a fundamental law of reality."

Wisdom marks the truth of suffering and leads to surrender. Surrender reveals both a sacred presence and a path. The sacred presence, already within us—almost like a pilot light—and the path to increasing its radiance are recognized as worthy of faith and confidence in a way nothing in the samsaric experience ever could be.

With direct personal experience of the four noble truths and the teachings on dependent arising—to whatever degree—we grow in both gratitude and authority. Brother David Steindl-Rast, the Catholic mystic, speaks of gratitude as "the wild joy of belonging..., our full appreciation of something altogether unearned, utterly gratuitous."

Pause for a moment, if you would, and consider the relationship of grace and gratitude. We experience gratitude when we recognize—through clear seeing—the value of that for which we feel grateful. Recognizing value, the heart naturally responds with trust, with confidence. We have a sense of an un-self-conscious certainty—the authority of the heart.

With growing insight, we are increasingly willing to trust in direct knowing—beyond conceptuality. We trust our own experiential realizations. At this juncture, Buddha said, we become "endowed with verified confidence in the Dharma."

As our appetite for "self" diminishes, our appetite for grace—for awakening—grows. The percentages shift gradually with the natural fading out of the worldly desire that arises with seeing. We increasingly turn to grace as the only fully adequate, fully appropriate experience of being. We are no longer willing to implode pure awareness by placing an "I" in it.

Our essential nature, at the level of the heart, recognizes itself as grace. Grace has known that all along. We begin to let the divine spark within us, abiding at the level of the heart, express itself. From thirteenth-century mystic poet Kabir come the words: "the damage I have done to myself fades, / a million suns come forward with light, / when I sit firmly in that world."

Rather than viewing surrender as "giving up," we come to recognize it as an acknowledgment of our willingness, our longing, to participate in grace's unfolding of us. We each can begin a beautiful, improvisational dance with the sacred—mindfully surrendering the need to identify with, grasp onto, or push away. We recognize surrender as a sacrament.

A sacrament is an acknowledgment of the sacred, a bow to the holy. A sacrament honors the truth that is always already so. The sacrament of surrender honors the truth of our essential nature.

Try this practice of surrender, if you like. Pause and quiet. Dedicate about fifteen minutes to simply surrender any inclination to allow attention to follow or enter into the "I"-thoughts that arise. Just surrender each inclination. Surrender whatever feels like a "need" to believe in the identity. Surrender the comfort of the familiarity of the thought. Surrender the habituated ignorance that has assented to the truth of the "I"-illusion this great, long time.

Over and over, surrender the inclination to follow a thought, to identify with it. Surrender hope and habituation. Surrender the "need" and "want" thoughts. Surrender the "I"-thought. Recognize surrender as a willingness. Recognize grace's part in establishing that willingness within us. It is a willingness to surrender every inclination to fuel the "I"-illusion.

You will note a growing lightness of being with each deliberate moment of surrender, a growing absorption in silence, a growing awareness of the contentment ever present in awareness, in grace. You will notice, as you engage in this practice, that attention shifts to the level of the heart. Drop by drop, each time we engage the "gesture of surrender," as Christian mystic Cynthia Bourgeault calls it, attention returns to the heart, to natural great peace.

You can use imagery, if that's helpful. The act of surrender is like letting go of the string of a balloon. There is a release of attention from the balloon that might pull attention up and away—out of here, out of now. Our center of gravity shifts from the head to the heart, from conceptuality to direct seeing, from chatter to silence, from the unease of grasping to contented peace.

The sacrament of surrender blesses us. It clears away, in each sacramental act, our obstructions to grace. We enter presence with innocence, a naked and undefended stance without the armor of self-reference, agenda, or conceptuality. We come to know grace when we come with no adornment—no mental images, no ideas. As Catholic mystic James Finley observed, "No idea of God is God. No idea of you is you."

IN BUDDHISM, this extinguishing of attention's desire to remain bound within samsara is called *renunciation*. As our attention is freed from enchantment, the seductive power of the system of self and suffering quiets. Whatever continued promises it makes—and the system will persist in promises, both whispered and shouted, for a long while—those promises are seen by discerning wisdom as empty, as unreliable, as potentially enslaving. As we renounce—which is to say, as we surrender—we awaken from samsara's trance.

You may recall the Tibetan word for grasping, *shenpa*. The word for renunciation—or surrender—is *shenlok*. The root word of both of them, *shen*, has to do with passion. Our English word, *passion*, comes from the Latin root word for suffering. Passion controls attention. Dispassion frees it. Buddha advised us many times that through dispassion we are released from suffering.

There is no loss of joy or love or individual flavor when we engage in such a practice of moment-by-moment surrender. In surrendering, the innate qualities of our essential nature—the noble qualities—intensify. Joy, love, and the individual flavor we were created to express mature and ripen when the obstruction of self is removed.

Established in Being, we increasingly live in an unselfconscious contentedness. Happiness is a natural state. We land in it when we offer our willingness for the illusion to die on the vine. You will witness that *not* following compulsions is a great act of self-compassion.

Meeting the present moment as it is, we find a tranquil composure—craving, grasping, "wanting" nothing. There is less and less "self" to "want." We begin to participate in our own illumination.

In silence—toward the end of life, in retreat, in our sustained and committed practice, and in our frequent pausing—we simply allow the momentum of fabrications to wash over us, surrendering any habitual impulse to follow the waves out to sea. Surrender returns us to silence and silence is a transformative field. No chatter, no self.

With each momentary release of the inessential, we give up on becoming anything other than who we are at essence—letting "no false gods before us." Self-surrender is a mystic's path, a path utterly aligned with a mystic's longing, an endless sacrament.

Surrender is a practice we can engage all day long. We can do it on the golf course, at the red light, in the kitchen, in the office. We certainly practice the sacrament of surrender as we sit in formal practice—surrendering the inclination to follow each wandering thought as it arises, surrendering the identification with "I," the one who is meditating. Each release leads to a more essential distillation of our experience of being. Each gesture validates the sacred, ever present within and around.

A. H. Almaas calls the state of authentic, awakened being "so present that you're gone." Ram Dass speaks of the joy of "nobody home."

Each of us has the potential to become *tathāgata*, a Sanskrit word meaning "thus come, thus gone." It is our birthright. Every awakened being who has gone before us is inviting us, encouraging us, urging us to claim that birthright.

26

Resting at the Heart

TOGETHER WE'VE EXPLORED each of the twelve conditions of dependent arising, just as Keith Jarrett explored the eighty-eight keys of a piano. We've come to know them.

We've explored their universal patterns, as well as investigated and witnessed the unique way the universal patterns arise in our own minds. We've taken the opportunities to witness their dynamics and to observe their power to bind our attention within them. We've observed how the dynamics create the exact same "I"-sense, a harmonic of these universal dynamics, in each of our unique manifestations.

To whatever degree of depth each of us has done so, we've made many of the realizations Buddha shared our own. We've at least had powerful glimpses of them. We've used his teachings as a template for seeing, leading to both an increased understanding of these previously unexamined dynamics and a diminished inclination to live our lives unmindfully.

Without mindfulness, we relied on conceptuality, the mistaken conclusions of ignorance, habit, and desire. Buddha offered a scaffolding to climb up on as we grow into the truth of who we are. Intimately contemplating the insights of Buddha's realized awareness, we've refined the subtlety of our seeing and understanding. We've begun to dissolve the tight grip of the sense of self. Buddha offered a finger pointing in a wise direction, a shoulder to stand on. His framework has led us, and can continue to lead us, to increasingly profound levels of understanding.

We've come closer to the truth of things. We've come closer to the ever-presence of grace and have grown in our capacity to recognize it. We've grown in our faith, our confidence in grace's cooperation with our longing to awaken. Grace's cooperation and our longing to awaken are not two different things. Grace "dis-appears" our shadowed thoughts, our images of smallness and separation, in its radiance.

We've come to trust inquiry, the clear seeing of wisdom, and come to recognize its power to dilute the power of ignorance. As we've stared down any one of the links or conditions, we've seen wisdom's capacity to free attention from the thrall of all the conditioned assumptions.

We've examined *ignorance* as the inclination to turn away, as the ground environment that allows all the impersonal processes of dependent arising to ensnare attention without our even noticing. We have seen how the simple question, what is looking—ignorance or wisdom, self or grace?, has such transformative force. And, in any moment, we are increasingly able and willing to surrender the thoughts, inclinations, and habituations when we recognize that ignorance has been steering the ship.

We've looked at *karmic formations*, recognizing not only the universal karmic formation of clinging to a self but also the particular flavor and leanings of our own unique karmic formations. We've also seen that who we are is not our habit patterns. There is no need to carry either pride or shame about them. We only need mindfulness in service to awakening.

Pausing to reflect, to see, has allowed us to recognize the influence of the condition, *consciousness*. We're more aware of its quick jump to conclusions, its rush to provide a seeming continuity to whatever it is that we label "I" and "me." Pausing, we've experienced the gaps of stillness between the moments of assumption, the gaps of wordlessness between the moments of definition.

We have come to recognize those gaps as the very essence of the present moment, the very essence of grace, and an invitation into awareness beyond self. Contemplative poet Jan Richardson recognizes the gaps as the opportunities to "open our eyes,/to learn to see/ what has forever/shimmered in front of us." In Tibetan Buddhism, those gaps are called *bodhimaṇḍalas*, the ever-present invitation and opportunity to awaken.

We have a new lightness with *name-and-form*, recognizing label as simple convenience in the conventional world of appearances. We can now increasingly go through the world, go through our day, understanding that label need not proclaim the inherent existence of any phenomena. That new lightness is enlivening, refreshing, and freeing. It offers a radically new view.

In our contemplation and reflection, we've come to see the survival benefit of both the *six senses* and *contact*. We've also come to see how the simple survival benefit can be expropriated by the samsaric cycle. Without mindfulness, our entire survival imperative ends up in service to ego rather than simply in service to the protection and viability of our physical existence.

We've grown in our understanding that the very nature of human sense organs limits us to only selected ranges of appearances. The seen world lies between pure light and pure darkness. Such an understanding contributes to our growing inclination to question the authority of our unexamined assumptions. We've practiced remaining "at the sense gates," thus allowing the inflow of sensory data to be closer to the truth of the way things are than the distorted mental images we hold would have us assume.

We've become familiar with the spontaneous arising of *feeling* upon contact. We've diminished the "Dharma lag" between the arising of feeling positive, negative, or neither-positive-nor-negative and our recognition of it.

Our inquiry into the conditions of dependent arising as they operate in our own minds has led us to recognize the arising of "I" with the arising of "want." Through contemplation and investigation, we have seen the quick rush feeling takes into *craving* and on into *grasping*. We have watched our attention become hijacked. The hijackers move it instantly to *becoming*, the desire to be someone, the need to be an "I."

We've watched the quick turn into *birth* and the inevitable conclusion of *aging-and-death*, or suffering. And we've seen that, unless we apply mindfulness—an interest and curiosity about what is happening—attention is haphazardly spun around again with the next cycle to be thrashed once more with suffering—gross or subtle. Curiosity can supersede the urgent need for satisfaction. It may have killed a cat—but it can save us.

Mindfully, we can use any of the conditioning factors that once kept us bound in service to unbinding. We can repurpose them. We can use the power of intention within karmic formations, for example, changing the nature and the groove of our habits, carving out a new "line of least resistance." Our new line of least resistance begins to incline naturally and spontaneously toward grace.

We can rededicate our becoming from one of self-reference to one of self-surrender. We surrender the inclination to follow the pull of craving and grasping, and note the spacious freedom and steady balance of equanimity, when we do so. We can make good use of name-and-form, using it to work for us. We do this when we recognize a label as simply a "correct" apprehension of an appearance rather than a mistaken declaration about the nature of its existence. We can repurpose name-and-form when we simply recognize tension, confusion, and complicated storylines as "ignorance"—and let go of it. We have recognized ignorance as entrapment, an endlessly circling dead end.

We repurpose when we employ each moment of pausing, contemplation, and the inner silence of absorption to halt the rush of conditions as well as to request the blessing of grace's cooperation in our unbinding. The conscious use of any one of the conditions—an option available from the stance of wisdom—can free attention from the entire system, releasing the eddy into the divine flow.

We've worked with the scaffolding Buddha offered for the refinement of our seeing, our ways of knowing, our sense of identity. It has brought us to a more subtly attuned, more clear-seeing, more mindful and heartful level of awareness. It has allowed us to recognize the "I"-illusion as illusion, as harmonic or overtone of the entire spinning system. It has allowed us to recognize the suffering that arises inevitably with "self." It has brought us face to face with the noble truths and our own essential nature.

WITH WHATEVER DEGREE of diligence we have applied to contemplating Buddha's teachings, we have come closer to the truth. Although approaching truth is often painful, there is less suffering closer to the truth. Life becomes more manageable, our moment-by-moment experience more sane, more compassionate, more balanced in equanimity.

Buddha's teachings have allowed us to recognize the three marks of existence—suffering, impermanence, and emptiness—not as beliefs to adopt but truths we're invited to experience. Recognizing the three marks of existence is important—they're like the trail markers in the dense woods along the Appalachian Trail. They're slashed into trees to keep us on the right path, pointing in the right direction.

The first mark is suffering, dukkha. Existence in a world bound only by form, limited only to self—samsara—is characterized by suffering. We can recall all the time in our lives we've spent worrying, lamenting, wishing, planning, hiding, preening, defending, manipulating, and denying. We can ask ourselves where has all that exertion of energy brought us? Has it brought us any closer to knowing the holiness of our own essential nature?

The second mark or characteristic of existence is impermanence. With our understanding of dependent arising, we've come to realize that all appearances rise and fall, emerge and dissolve. There is, in the world of form, no permanently appearing phenomenon. There is nothing that will not, like water, run through our grasp. No relationship, no happiness, no experience, no achievement or renown, no possession or physical body will permanently endure. The denial of impermanence is a cause of suffering.

It was Homer who said, "As is the generation of leaves, so is that of men." Impermanence is the nature of all compounded things—scarlet maple leaves, our beloveds, ourselves. The realization of impermanence, *anicca* in Pali, has vast implications—including, of course, the fact of our mortality. All things tend toward their ruin.

We miss tens of thousands of momentary opportunities to cultivate gratitude and appreciation for the unique singularity of each never-before, never-again arising when—clinging—we ignore impermanence. The seventeenth-century Buddhist poet Basho speaks of an ephemeral moment at the cutting edge of grace's newest unfolding:

> the old pond;
> a frog jumps in
> —the sound of water.

Basho was present in that singular passing "now." We, too often, miss the moment when we cover it with a memory. We miss the majesty and mystery of immediacy when we try to grab a memento of it to keep for the future instead of simply entering it. We miss now. We miss all that now offers—the timeless universality Basho entered.

Our whole lives have been witness to impermanence. Usually we notice only impermanence's most graphic illustrations, such as ending a relationship or losing a job or breaking a teapot. Yet impermanence proceeds endlessly and subtly. Nagarjuna, a third-century Indian Buddhist master, observed, "Life is so fragile, no more than a bubble blown to and fro in the wind. How astonishing to think that after an out-breath there will be an in-breath, or that we will awaken after a night's sleep."

We can ask ourselves what do I do to try to halt the ceaseless flow of endlessly changing appearances? How am I ignoring or resisting impermanence? What remains when I can no longer deny impermanence? We can rest in what remains.

The third mark of existence, as Buddha shared from his realized awareness and as we ourselves have come to recognize, is emptiness, *anattā* in Pali. Emptiness does not mean nothingness. If there were such a word as "no-thing-ness," that word would come closer to the meaning. Emptiness refers to the absence of inherent, separate existence of any phenomenon, including the phenomenon we identify as self.

Emptiness refers to the sacred formless, to the fullness of unobstructed Being in display, to wondrous and infinite and interconnected potential.

All who look deeply enough come to the same realization. Thomas Keating expressed it this way: "Everything . . . just is; always changing, becoming something new; always together with everything else; dependent and interconnected; differentiating yet always the same; fusing, oneing, never still, always in relationship to everything."

Nothing exists independently of immeasurable causes and conditions, as we've each also come to see. We have looked at that together since the first eddy metaphor. The truth is of interdependence, interbeing. What is so is an endless, interconnected display of grace. Insight into emptiness highlights and deepens our awe and gratitude for this Great Mystery. It nurtures an increasing conscientiousness and compassion and reverence for all that, before any degree of awakening, we had considered as "other." We can ask ourselves, where do I place the boundaries of "me"?

If you like, take the time to engage in a practice of imagination. Imagine your body expanding to the size of the universe, expanding to the end of the cosmos and beyond. In this imagining, we recognize that the space between the atoms of our body, even the space between the subatomic particles of each atom of our body, is vast. Stunningly vast space.

And ask—where is "I" to be found in this vast and shimmering space? Where is its location? Where are its boundaries? Stay with the questions for a bit and simply allow the grasping of conceptions to fall away. Surrender them. Again, where is "I" to be found in this vast and shimmering space? And rest for a while in that sacred emptiness, the formless interbeing of all appearances in form.

Even in this moment, as we breathe in oxygen molecules a million others have breathed before us, as teeming civilizations of microbes and bacteria and viruses—each with their own evolutionary agenda—live within these bodies we claim as our own, even as we exchange molecules with the earth every time our feet touch the ground, even as we recognize our flesh and bones to be made of the same material as stars that were born thousands of light years ago, even in this moment—can I still claim "I" as separate?

It is a relief and a release to let go of "self," to let go into interbeing, to practice the self-surrender that characterizes us as mystics and illuminates our being in communion.

Thomas Merton let go into the stunning realization of interbeing. He described the experience as "Waking from a dream of separateness. . . . This sense of liberation from all illusory difference was such a relief and such a joy that I almost laughed out loud." He had that realization standing on the corner of Fourth and Walnut in Louisville, Kentucky on his way to a hardware store—as ordinary a spot as Basho's old pond.

Grace is here. Grace is now. It is not other than who we are. It is not hidden away. It is the ground of every ordinary moment, a truth we come to know for ourselves when we free attention from the spinning cobwebs that have bound it. We come to know grace when we actually show up. Laughing out loud, the lion's roar—they both arise with the same realization.

The realization of the three marks of existence is the fruit of our inquiry into the four noble truths and our careful and diligent investigation of the conditions of dependent arising. The scaffolding Buddha provided led us to this meaningful juncture. By meaningful juncture, I'm referring to the expanded sense of being and the growing wisdom we've begun to embody following Buddha's "pointing out instructions." Assisted by grace, we've been blessed—to whatever degree—with a transformative shift into a larger experience of life, a more helpful stance vis-à-vis awakening. This meaningful juncture is not an "end spot," however, but a fruitful spot for ever-deepening realization—the very nature of awakening.

We can respect where our practice has brought us. When we clearly see all of the conditions and their spinning, mutually influencing interactions, we no longer resurrect the past and overlay it upon the present. Even abandoning our passion for any one of the conditions, we begin to free the future from this wheel of unease, from self and suffering.

Buddha called the mind that has come to the end of craving "totally unbound." We are fortunate beyond imagining to have these tools. We simply cooperate with grace in our practice, recognizing that grace longs for our unbinding as much as we do.

In the Dhammapada, Buddha gave voice to his experience of inquiring into the conditions of dependent arising. He said, "Through the round of many births I roamed without reward, without rest, seeking the house-builder. Painful is birth again and again. House-builder, you're seen! You will not build a house again. All your rafters are broken, the ridge pole destroyed, gone to the Unformed, the mind has come to the end of craving." This is the profundity to which inquiry into the nature of self and suffering can lead us.

Again, blessed be the explorer. Blessed be the lover of truth, the precious human being with an opening heart.

FROM THIS MEANINGFUL JUNCTURE—arrived at with a deepened understanding of the noble truths and of the cycle of self and suffering—let's turn our attention now to one of Buddha's most well-known teachings. These are the teachings of the Heart Sutra. The Heart Sutra is referred to by Buddhist teachers and practitioners as a wisdom teaching. In the teaching, Avalokiteshvara, the enlightened embodiment of compassion, symbolically speaks for Buddha. The symbolism is deep and purposeful—a powerful reminder that profound wisdom only arises with profound compassion. Each demands the other. Each bows to the other.

In the Perfection of Wisdom teachings of which the Heart Sutra is a part, Buddha compassionately passes us a live grenade. The Heart Sutra has the potential to explode everything we've ever unmindfully thought—every dualistic notion, every mistaken assumption, every presumed certitude.

Buddha completely and utterly destroys the scaffolding of his teachings that we've been mindfully using throughout our exploration. He throws us into chaos with the Heart Sutra teachings, a chaos that will lead ultimately—if we stay open to it—to a surrender of our present understanding and to an inclusive transcendence of it in an ongoing leap of ever-deepening realization.

The Heart Sutra takes the four noble truths and the twelve conditions we've studied with such diligence—that inquiry having led to a deeper, more subtle awareness and a wispier sense of self—and completely blows up the ground beneath our feet.

In pointing us toward onward and deeper, the Heart Sutra has this to say about all we've been exploring, contemplating, and working with:

"All experience is emptiness. It is not defined. It is not born or destroyed, impure or free from impurity, not incomplete or complete."
"In emptiness, there is no ignorance, no end of ignorance up to old

age and death, no end of old age and death, no suffering, no origin,
no cessation, no path, no pristine awareness, no attainment, and
no non-attainment."

This is the teaching of the Heart Sutra as it relates to dependent arising, that helpful template for seeing. There is no ignorance, karmic formations, consciousness, name-and-form, or six senses. Nor is there an end to ignorance, karmic formations, consciousness, name-and-form, or six senses. "There is no eye, no ear, no nose, no tongue, no body, no mentality; no form, no sound, no smell, no taste, no tactile object, no phenomenon," the Heart Sutra proclaims. There is no contact, feeling, craving, grasping, becoming, birth, aging-and-death. Nor is there no end of any of them. As for the four noble truths, those fruitful, beneficial guides for our journey, the Heart Sutra teaches "there is no suffering, no origin, no cessation, and no path."

The Heart Sutra pulls the rug out from under the entire framework with which we've been sincerely engaged and the understanding we've come to as a consequence. It boggles the mind.

It's meant to boggle the mind. It's "crazy wisdom," as Chögyam Trungpa and plenty of love-drunk Sufi mystics called clear seeing. It is utterly beyond the grasp of our logical, dualistic, conceptual minds. This is by design.

After all our devotion to understanding Buddha's teachings, the Heart Sutra can leave us totally uncomprehending, completely stunned.

We have already worked with diligence to decipher and unpack Buddha's cryptic dependent arising teachings, "When this appears, that appears. When this ceases, that ceases." We have already applied our attention and worked with the scaffolding of "when this, then that." It has led us to more subtle understanding and increased unbinding.

Now we are asked to approach "there is no this, there is no end of this; there is no that, there is no end of that." Even approaching the words leaves the conceptual mind scratching its head and going, "Huh?!"

Thich Nhat Hanh calls the Heart Sutra "the insight that takes us to the other shore." We have realized at this point in our spiritual path that Buddha's insight will not take us to the "other shore." Only when the insight is our own, when it dawns in our own awareness, does the insight take us to the other shore.

What are we to do as the framework with which we've been working is exploded and we're flung into the profundity of emptiness? Buddha suggests we "consider holding on to nothing."

All the conditions—from ignorance to aging-and-death—and all of the noble truths—from the first to the fourth—are fabricated steps of a constructed, albeit helpful, scaffolding for our exploration. Rafts to use to cross the river. As with all constructed things, it is impermanent and, ultimately, empty. And so it is with everything else we cling to, have ever clung to, or might cling to—every scaffolding.

WE CAN'T APPROACH the teaching with conceptual mind. "Maybe I can diagram it, sketch it out in a chart." "Maybe I can read that one more book that might give the answer." "Maybe I can just think harder." It's not hard to imagine that any of these thoughts might arise in our minds as possible strategies. We so want to "figure it out." The conceptual mind, the mind trapped in samsara, is itself the interference pattern blocking the truth, blocking grace. The conceptual mind has no capacity for the comprehension—the realization—of this teaching.

The Heart Sutra leads us to—and beyond—the limit of conceptuality's capacity and functioning. The conceptual mind boggles with paradox. Conceptual mind works with mental images of what's arising. Conceptual mind holds itself at a dualistic remove and is incapable of holding two contradictory mental images simultaneously. It short circuits with this teaching. The Heart Sutra is intended to short circuit conceptual mind. Conceptual mind is not adequate to the task of realization.

It has been said many times that paradox is how the truth appears to the conceptual mind. Our conceptual minds will never, ever be able to realize "there is no this, there is no that. There is no end to this, there is no end to that." "This" and "that" are the very building blocks of conceptuality's—which is to say, samsara's—paradigm. Take them away and the bottom falls out of the bucket.

WHAT CAN WE DO with this teaching? What can we do with the insights from the Heart Sutra? There is nothing *to do*. There is only surrender.

When we recognize conceptuality's limitations, we can begin to more easily surrender our attachment to it. When we recognize conceptuality's limitations, we realize that conceptuality does not *participate* in what's arising. Conceptuality is at a remove from the reality of each moment in the same way that a definition of ice cream is at a remove from the taste of it. We grow in our understanding that a participatory stance in grace arises from the heart.

We don't have to recognize conceptuality's limitations completely and utterly, all at once. We will, no doubt, turn to it or fall back into it ten thousand times more. But every time we look from wisdom at conceptuality's limitations, we let go. A small drop of attention falls into the flame at the heart and the light shines more brightly; the illumination of our being increases, radiance grows—as does wisdom.

Every time we surrender, we land in the heart. There is nowhere else to go. The heart is life unshaped by mind, free from conditioning, a clarity capable of direct experiential realization.

THE HEART SUTRA is wonderfully named. It is a call to the heart, a call to leave our life-long residence in conceptual mind, the home of ignorance, self, and suffering. It is a call to utter surrender. What appears paradoxical to conceptual mind is simply and wordlessly known when we land and rest in the groundless ground of the heart.

The mind may boggle upon confrontation with the Heart Sutra—or any profound reference to the mystery of truth. But the universe is openly and freely displayed before and within us. The universe isn't designed, so that the recognition of ever-present grace will be tricky or complex or bewildering. Any trickiness, complexity, or bewilderment we experience in our relationship with grace comes from ignorance. We have been looking for truth with the wrong tool, the wrong lens. The universe isn't trying to put us through a grueling test to certify our eligibility to embrace the truth and be embraced by it. Grace isn't trying to see if we can ace a complicated exam before it offers truth, wisdom, and compassion as reward. Grace longs for the return of our wandering attention.

In fact, grace—recognizing that we don't live that long—has made awakening simple, dropping hints all over the place.

The hints have been here all the while. Jesus told us to love one another. Avalokiteshvara, the pure and beautiful enlightened embodiment of compassion, is the one scrambling our conceptual mind as he delivers the wisdom teaching of the Heart Sutra. That is no accident.

If there were a chorus of every awakened being, the song sung would be love, would be kindness, would be compassion, would be gratitude. Every teacher has pointed to the heart—the Sacred Heart, the Heart Jewel, and other such names. It has always and only been our heart resonating in the most meaningful and profound moments of our lives, always and only been our heart worthy of trust.

The teaching of the Heart Sutra only seems crazy and incomprehensible to conceptual mind. It is only understandable by the heart.

We all came supplied with a "heart center," so not one of us is at a disadvantage. Landing in our own true nature is meant to be easy. It's meant to be simple. It's right here, right now and always has been. Lay down the self and the assumptions and all the rest of the baggage. Come down into the heartmind. Recognize it—it has a warmth and a radiance. Trust it—it is a truth-seer and a truth-teller. Abide in it—it is our own home, our essential nature.

We're the ones who have been making landing in the heart difficult by insisting on using conceptual mind, an aspect of the system of suffering, as the only means at our disposal. Reliance upon conceptual mind is what is to be surrendered. We've begun to do that. And we've begun to recognize that our surrender of blind conceptual reliance leads us directly to the heart.

I HAVE SAID ELSEWHERE that the three great tasks of a human life are confronting our mortality, stilling the mind, and opening the heart. When we confront our mortality, we live with greater mindfulness, appreciation, urgency, and presence. When we empty the mind of all the strands of its web of "this" and "that," the bottom falls out. Our binding conceptual paradigm has nothing left holding it up. When the bottom falls out, we land in the heart. We land in what we've been looking for.

We can think of the heart, the subtle energy center in the very center of our chest, as a point of balance, as a center of nonconceptual knowing, the abode of the transcendent within the immanence of our living individual manifestation. As the great Catholic mystic Pierre Teilhard de Chardin said, "The stuff of the universe is spirit-matter." Soul—the heartmind, the abode of love, is the middle way—our resting place in "spirit-matter," midway between the particular and the Absolute, open to both.

At first, as we land in the heart, we may well feel sorrow. There is so much sorrow in the world. We begin to be with it and in it, genuinely open to the experience of sorrow. Sorrow is waterlogged with the tears of the world. Maybe we need to feel the unbearable pain of the world breaking our heart open before we can bow before the unbearable beauty.

Sorrow is not a jagged emotion; it's a releasing one, a cleansing one, almost a rain-washing one. Jesus noted, "From their innermost being will flow rivers of living water." The heart is softened in this opening. The knots around the heart—all that binding—come undone. We become boundaryless, undefended, open, peaceful, and powerful. We become compassionate as the heart center blazes in wisdom, recognizing its own true nature and the true nature of every "other."

We can think of the heart center as the zero point between a vertical dimension of the sacred and a horizontal dimension of a "self," the point of their intersection. This is the point of balance, at zero, wanting nothing, resisting nothing. This zero point is the point of balance where the realization rests that we are not other than grace in one of its wondrous millions of manifestations of majesty and mystery.

To me, the most beautiful lines in the Heart Sutra are: "Form is empty; emptiness is form. Emptiness is not other than form; form also is not other than emptiness." This form I have called "me" is not other than grace. Nor is the form you call "you." These eddies are not other than water.

Unbound, at the heart, we rest in the middle ground between our human nature and our Buddha nature—embracing it all, embraced by it all. Thomas Keating described this as "a certain openness to being everything and nothing, both at once and in all that is in-between. This is God in us and we in God." To recall an earlier insight, we can rest in the truth that, in this very moment, grace is Kathleen-ing, grace is fill-in-your-name-ing. To rest in that truth is to rest in soul—"everything and nothing, both at once and in all that is in-between."

Unbound, at the heart, we remain in equanimity, poised like Green Tara, the enlightened embodiment of service in Tibetan iconography—with one leg in meditation posture, the other extended to respond to suffering beings. We remain in equanimity, poised between contemplation and action.

We remain at the zero point, recognizing the illusoriness of this dream within a dream while simultaneously recognizing our radical accountability for our actions of body, speech, and mind within the dream. The wisdom that realizes emptiness also realizes compassion.

As Buddhist teacher Matthew Flickstein puts it, "Compassion is the willingness to play in the field of dreams even though you are awake."

Unbound, we can live the life we were born for, bringing to a suffering world the unique offering of an awakened individual manifestation of grace. In this very moment, our hearts are calling us home to rest in the truth.

The great Indian mystic, Paramahansa Yogananda, composed a chant that has been sung, often through the night, in villages and temples in India, on rocky cliffs above the Pacific Ocean, in the alpine meadows of the Sangre de Cristo and Rocky Mountains, and in clearings in the New England woods. "Listen, listen, listen to my heart song. I will never forget you. I will never forsake you."

Who is singing—
grace singing to soul
or soul singing to grace?
It is one voice.
Listen.

ACKNOWLEDGMENTS

THIS BOOK WAS A JOY TO WRITE. I'm grateful for the privilege and am hopeful that it will also be a joy to read and contemplate.

Deepest bow of respect to Rodney Smith. His insight into "self" as a harmonic inspired me. He opened my mind and heart to these teachings and to the necessity of owning our own path as grace leads us to it and through it.

Deep endless bow of gratitude to the rich, loving blessing of my family—each and every one of you. You blow me away.

ABOUT THE AUTHOR

KATHLEEN DOWLING SINGH is a Dharma practitioner and in-demand speaker and teacher. She is the author of *The Grace in Dying: How We Are Transformed Spiritually as We Die; The Grace in Aging: Awaken as You Grow Older*; and *The Grace in Living: Recognize It, Trust It, Abide in It.* Kathleen lives in Sarasota, Florida.

She maintains a website at kathleendowlingsingh.com.

WHAT TO READ NEXT
FROM WISDOM PUBLICATIONS

THE GRACE IN AGING
Awaken as You Grow Older
Kathleen Dowling Singh

"Don't grow old without it." —Rachel Naomi Remen, MD, author of *Kitchen Table Wisdom*

THE GRACE IN LIVING
Recognize It, Trust It, Abide in It
Kathleen Dowling Singh

"Kathleen Dowling Singh has become one of the premier spiritual teachers of grace. We are quite impressed."—*Spirituality and Practice*

HOW TO WAKE UP
A Buddhist-Inspired Guide to Navigating Joy and Sorrow
Toni Bernhard

"This is a book for everyone."—Alida Brill, author of *Dancing at the River's Edge*

INTERCONNECTED
Embracing Life in Our Global Society
The Karmapa, Ogyen Trinley Dorje

"We are now so interdependent that it is in our own interest to take the whole of humanity into account. Hope lies with the generation who belong to the twenty-first century. If they can learn from the past and shape a different future, later this century the world could be a happier, more peaceful, and more environmentally stable place. I am very happy to see in this book the Karmapa Rinpoche taking a lead and advising practical ways to reach this goal."
—His Holiness the Dalai Lama

LIFE IS SPIRITUAL PRACTICE
Achieving Happiness with the Ten Perfections
Jean Smith

Discover the ten perfections—qualities of the heart and mind that cultivate happiness, wisdom, and compassion—and learn how to bring them into your life with this in-depth practice manual.

ENDING THE PURSUIT OF HAPPINESS
A Zen Guide
Barry Magid

"In an era dominated y the pursuit of quick fixes and the growing medicalization of the mental health field, this book provides a radical and vitally important challenge to the prevailing cultural ethos."
—Jeremy D. Safran, PhD, professor and director of clinical psychology, New School for Social Research, and editor of *Psychoanalysis and Buddhism*

About Wisdom Publications

Wisdom Publications is the leading publisher of classic and contemporary Buddhist books and practical works on mindfulness. To learn more about us or to explore our other books, please visit our website at wisdompubs.org or contact us at the address below.

Wisdom Publications
199 Elm Street
Somerville, MA 02144 USA

We are a 501(c)(3) organization, and donations in support of our mission are tax deductible.

Wisdom Publications is affiliated with the Foundation for the Preservation of the Mahayana Tradition (FPMT).